Event-Driven Architecture for Beginners using RabbitMQ and .NET

A comprehensive guide to distributed solutions with RabbitMQ and .NET

Abhisek Sinha

www.bpbonline.com

First Edition 2024

ISBN: 978-93-5551-692-3

Distributors:

BPB PUBLICATIONS
20, Ansari Road, Darya Ganj
New Delhi-110002
Ph: 23254990/23254991

DECCAN AGENCIES
4-3-329, Bank Street,
Hyderabad-500195
Ph: 24756967/24756400

MICRO MEDIA
Shop No. 5, Mahendra Chambers,
150 DN Rd. Next to Capital Cinema,
V.T. (C.S.T.) Station, MUMBAI-400 001
Ph: 22078296/22078297

To View Complete BPB Publications Catalogue Scan the QR Code:

Published by Manish Jain for BPB Publications, 20 Ansari Road, Darya Ganj, New Delhi-110002 and Printed by him at Manipal Technologies, Manipal

www.bpbonline.com

Dedicated to

My daughter ***Aaranyaa,***

my wife ***Neeti***

and

my parents

About the Author

Abhisek Sinha boasts a robust career spanning over 18 years in the field of software development. Throughout this extensive journey, he has held pivotal roles as a technical leader and software engineer, contributing significantly to numerous projects. His expertise extends to delivering successful projects for major corporations. Notably, he has been instrumental in the accomplishment of projects across diverse geographical landscapes, including India, Singapore, and Australia.

Currently, Abhisek serves as a Software Architecture Specialist and a Technical Advisor at Westpac Ltd, a leading Australian bank. His role in such a prominent institution underscores his depth of knowledge and practical experience in the software development domain.

Abhisek is not only a seasoned professional but also an accomplished postgraduate, having completed a degree in Information Technology. Additionally, he holds a Bachelor's degree in Computer Applications with a specialization in Agile Methods.

In recognition of his commitment to excellence in enterprise architecture, Abhisek has successfully obtained TOGAF Certification. This credential signifies his proficiency in navigating the complexities of enterprise-level architecture.

Beyond his corporate contributions, Abhisek actively engages with the global IT community. He shares his insights and experiences as a speaker in international IT conferences, offering valuable perspectives on industry trends and best practices. Furthermore, he contributes to the body of knowledge in software development by writing technical articles, with a focus on Web Development and related topics.

Abhisek Sinha's multifaceted background and wealth of experience make him a valuable contributor to the evolving landscape of software development, and his insights permeate the content of this book, enriching the reader's understanding of event-driven architecture using RabbitMQ and .NET.

About the Reviewer

Romain Ottonelli Dabadie is a seasoned technical expert and .NET enthusiast, who forged his experience in the IT landscape of France and Canada. With over a decade of experience, he's a trusted professional, excelling in crafting robust solutions using .NET with a strong background in distributed systems with RabbitMQ among others. Romain's journey includes diverse roles, mostly in the financial and energy domains, showcasing a commitment to excellence. Beyond his technical prowess, Romain actively engages on social media, sharing insights with the tech community. He stays abreast of Microsoft's latest developments, demonstrating a keen interest in their news and advancements.

Acknowledgement

I want to express my deepest gratitude to my family and friends for their unwavering support and encouragement throughout this book's writing.

I am also grateful to BPB Publications for their guidance and expertise in bringing this book to fruition. It was a long journey of revising this book, with valuable participation and collaboration of reviewers, technical experts, and editors.

I would also like to acknowledge the valuable contributions of my colleagues and co-worker during my many years working in the tech industry. They have taught me so much and have provided valuable feedback on my work.

Finally, I would like to thank all the readers who have taken an interest in my book, and making it a reality. Your encouragement has been invaluable.

Preface

Welcome to the immersive world of event-driven architecture (EDA) using RabbitMQ and .NET! This book is crafted to be your definitive guide in mastering the intricacies of building robust and scalable applications through the lens of event-driven systems.

Our journey begins by exploring the core principles of event-driven architecture, where RabbitMQ takes center stage as a potent message broker. We aim to provide a solid foundation for developers new to EDA, offering insights into creating applications that seamlessly respond to events.

As we explore the specifics of event-driven systems, we leverage the capabilities of the .NET platform to craft applications that are not only efficient and reliable but also easy to maintain. Through this exploration, you will gain a comprehensive understanding of how .NET complements the event-driven paradigm.

Throughout the book, we discuss best practices and design patterns tailored to the unique demands of event-driven architecture. Real-world examples are generously shared, offering practical insights to reinforce your understanding of these crucial concepts.

This book is designed for developers eager to delve into the practical aspects of event-driven architecture using RabbitMQ and .NET. Whether you are starting your journey in enterprise development or a seasoned professional aiming to enhance your expertise, the content presented here is geared to be both informative and applicable.

By the conclusion of this exploration, you will possess the knowledge and skills required to navigate the realm of event-driven architecture using RabbitMQ and .NET. Embrace the future of application development with confidence, armed with the insights and practices outlined in this book.

I sincerely hope this guide proves to be a valuable companion on your path to mastering event-driven architecture. Let the adventure commence!

Chapter 1: The Realization and Significance of Event-Driven Architecture – This chapter delves into the fundamentals of event-driven systems, comparing them to conventional architectures. It also covers the key concepts and principles that define EDA, including event sourcing, event-driven microservices, and event-driven data management.

Chapter 2: Core Concepts of Event-Driven Architecture – This chapter will explore the basic concepts and principles that serve as the foundation of event-driven architecture. Gaining a deep understanding of these concepts is crucial for creating systems that depend on event-driven architecture. Thus, it is important to grasp these concepts thoroughly to develop successful event-driven systems.

Chapter 3: Designing Event-Driven Systems – In the chapter, you will discover how to create a strong event-driven system through design and implementation. You will learn how to identify which events to produce and consume, how to create a schema, an event bus, and other critical components to create an event driven system.

Chapter 4: RabbitMQ for Event-Driven Microservices – In this chapter, we will walk you through the implementation of event-driven architecture using RabbitMQ messaging system and the .NET platform. It will provide a detailed insight into the functionalities and capabilities of RabbitMQ and .NET for developing event-driven systems. Following this implementation, you can create an event-driven system project in .NET with the help of RabbitMQ libraries.

Chapter 5: Building Event-Driven System with RabbitMQ and .NET – This chapter delves into the practical implementation of event-driven systems using RabbitMQ and .NET. It provides step-by-step instructions, code examples, and best practices for building event publishers, subscribers, and handlers. It demonstrates how to leverage RabbitMQ's messaging patterns and concepts within a .NET environment to create robust, scalable, event-driven architectures.

Chapter 6: Secure RabbitMQ Messaging with .NET– This chapter will delve into implementing essential security measures for event-driven systems. We will focus on authentication and authorization mechanisms to ensure the integrity and access control of event producers and consumers. Additionally, we will explore techniques for encrypting sensitive data within event payloads to protect sensitive information. Secure communication between event producers and consumers will also be discussed, along with implementing log aggregation and analysis for effective event tracing and auditing.

Chapter 7: Monitoring, Integration and Deployment in Event-Driven System – In this chapter, you will explore monitoring and management techniques, leveraging tools and libraries to ensure optimal performance and health of the event-driven system, while also managing RabbitMQ server and queues efficiently.

Chapter 8: Case Studies, Pitfalls and Future Horizons – In this chapter, we will explore real-world scenarios illustrating the impact of RabbitMQ and .NET in event-driven systems. Case studies will highlight the transformative effect of asynchronous messaging, emphasizing scalability and fault tolerance. We will delve into best practices, offering insights on performance optimization, caching, and load balancing for efficient event-driven architecture implementation. Additionally, common pitfalls in RabbitMQ and .NET within event-driven ecosystems will be scrutinized, with pragmatic strategies provided for readers to navigate challenges and craft resilient systems using these technologies.

Code Bundle and Coloured Images

Please follow the link to download the
Code Bundle and the *Coloured Images* of the book:

https://rebrand.ly/6a7intd

The code bundle for the book is also hosted on GitHub at
https://github.com/bpbpublications/Event-Driven-Architecture-for-Beginners-using-RabbitMQ-and-.NET
In case there's an update to the code, it will be updated on the existing GitHub repository.

We have code bundles from our rich catalogue of books and videos available at **https://github.com/bpbpublications**. Check them out!

Errata

We take immense pride in our work at BPB Publications and follow best practices to ensure the accuracy of our content to provide with an indulging reading experience to our subscribers. Our readers are our mirrors, and we use their inputs to reflect and improve upon human errors, if any, that may have occurred during the publishing processes involved. To let us maintain the quality and help us reach out to any readers who might be having difficulties due to any unforeseen errors, please write to us at :

errata@bpbonline.com

Your support, suggestions and feedbacks are highly appreciated by the BPB Publications' Family.

Did you know that BPB offers eBook versions of every book published, with PDF and ePub files available? You can upgrade to the eBook version at www.bpbonline.com and as a print book customer, you are entitled to a discount on the eBook copy. Get in touch with us at :

business@bpbonline.com for more details.

At **www.bpbonline.com**, you can also read a collection of free technical articles, sign up for a range of free newsletters, and receive exclusive discounts and offers on BPB books and eBooks.

Piracy

If you come across any illegal copies of our works in any form on the internet, we would be grateful if you would provide us with the location address or website name. Please contact us at **business@bpbonline.com** with a link to the material.

If you are interested in becoming an author

If there is a topic that you have expertise in, and you are interested in either writing or contributing to a book, please visit **www.bpbonline.com**. We have worked with thousands of developers and tech professionals, just like you, to help them share their insights with the global tech community. You can make a general application, apply for a specific hot topic that we are recruiting an author for, or submit your own idea.

Reviews

Please leave a review. Once you have read and used this book, why not leave a review on the site that you purchased it from? Potential readers can then see and use your unbiased opinion to make purchase decisions. We at BPB can understand what you think about our products, and our authors can see your feedback on their book. Thank you!

For more information about BPB, please visit **www.bpbonline.com**.

Table of Contents

Chapter 1
The Realization and Significance of Event-Driven Architecture

Introduction

Event-driven architecture (EDA) is a software design pattern that emphasizes the importance of events and reactions to those events in the design and development of software systems. This approach is gaining popularity in the software industry and differs from the traditional architecture centered on requests and responses. This chapter explores the fundamentals of event-driven systems, comparing them to conventional architectures. It also covers the key concepts and principles that define EDA, including event sourcing, event-driven microservices, and event-driven data management.

Structure

This chapter will cover the following topics:

- Event-driven architecture overview
- Advantages of EDA
- Challenges of EDA
- Comparing EDA with other architectural patterns
- Key components of EDA

- Common use cases for EDA
- Popular technologies and frameworks used in EDA

Objectives

This chapter is an introduction of yours to the world of EDA. You will be able to understand the basics of EDA. This is a tool to understand the core skills in event-driven architecture. It emphasizes mastery of the fundamentals, such as what event-driven architecture is, its importance in designing solutions, and what you will achieve if you implement event-driven architecture over other patterns.

Event-driven architecture overview

Event-driven architecture (EDA) is a design pattern in software engineering that enables software systems to respond to changes and events in real-time. EDA emphasizes creating, detecting, and utilizing events, resulting in highly flexible, scalable software systems that adapt to changing conditions.

An event in an event-driven architecture refers to a change or shift in a state that occurs when something changes or happens, which then triggers a subsequent action. This can be thought of as sending a message between different parts of a system to let them know that a change has occurred, and they should respond accordingly.

For instance, a user clicking a Submit button on a web page can initiate an action in a system. This action generates an event that triggers a series of events, such as data validation, database updates, and sending an email confirmation to the user. The event acts as a notification and travels through the architecture, coordinating the various components and ensuring that the intended actions are taken in response to the user's action.

The change of state in this scenario refers to the shift from an inactive state to an active state of the web form due to the user clicking the Submit button. This state change triggers a series of events that result in actions being taken within the system. The event serves as a notification of the change of state and ensures that the various components within the architecture respond accordingly.

In an EDA system, communication between components is achieved through events rather than relying on a central control mechanism to manage all operations. This approach reduces complexity and tight coupling between components, as each component only needs to respond to relevant events. This makes the system easier to manage and maintain, as each component only focuses on the important events.

Using events to communicate between components allows for greater scalability, as the system can easily respond to changing conditions and events. The event-driven approach to communication provides a flexible and scalable way to build software systems that can keep up with changes and events, making it a valuable tool for software engineers.

Overall, event-driven architecture is a design pattern that offers a flexible and scalable way to build software systems that can effectively respond to changing conditions and events. It reduces complexity and tight coupling between components, making managing and maintaining the system easier.

An event-driven design has makers who make a series of events and receivers who wait for these events.

Events are sent in real-time, allowing receivers to react to them as they happen promptly. A producer does not know which consumer is listening. The consumer of events is also decoupled from other consumers and witnesses to all the events produced. Refer to the following figure:

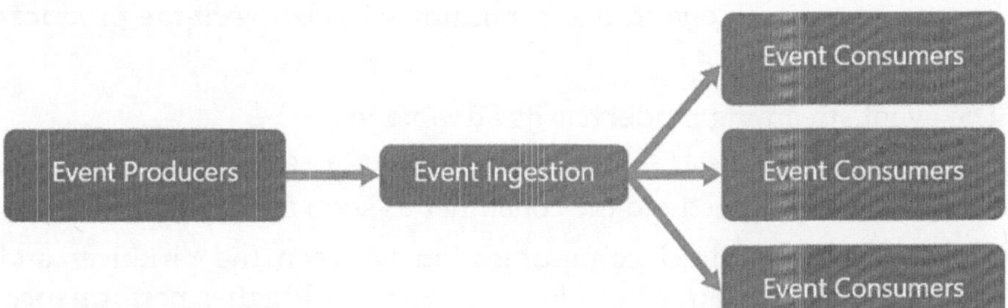

Figure 1.1: *Simple Event-Driven Architecture*

In an event-driven architecture, two main models manage events: the publisher/subscriber and event streaming models.

Publisher/subscriber

The publish/subscribe model involves using a central hub, a broker, to manage the flow of events. In this model, producers send events to the broker, and the broker broadcasts the events to all consumers that have expressed interest in the event. This allows multiple consumers to receive the same event, even though they may not know each other's existence. *ActiveMQ* and *RabbitMQ* are widely recognized brokers for the publish/subscribe pattern.

The publisher/subscriber model has its benefits, namely:

- Firstly, it decouples the event producers from the consumers, meaning that the producers do not need to know the specifics of who is receiving the events. This makes the architecture more flexible and scalable, as new consumers can be added or existing ones removed without affecting the producers.
- Secondly, the broker can filter and manipulate events before they are sent to consumers. This can be useful for logging, auditing, or transforming events into a different format.

Event streaming

The event streaming model is a more direct approach to managing events. This model sends events directly from the producer to the consumer. Consumers actively pull events from a stream, and they are sent to the specific consumer that has requested them. This model can be seen as a direct, one-to-one communication between the producer and the consumer.

The event streaming model has its advantages:

- Firstly, it allows for real-time processing of events, as the events are sent directly to the consumer as soon as they occur.
- Secondly, direct communication between the producer and consumer can lead to lower latency and higher performance, as the events do not need to pass through a central broker.
- Thirdly, the event stream model is well-suited to systems where the volume of events is low, as the overhead of a central broker can become a bottleneck in high-volume systems.

In conclusion, the choice between the publish/subscribe model and the event stream model depends on the specific requirements of the application being developed. Both models have their strengths and weaknesses. The best choice will depend on factors such as the volume of events, the real-time processing requirements, and the flexibility and scalability of the architecture.

When to use this architecture

The following are instances when you should use this architecture:

- **Microservices**: EDA is often used in microservice-based architectures, where multiple services must communicate to perform complex tasks. Events allow services to be decoupled and to work independently while communicating effectively.
- **Internet of Things (IoT)**: In IoT systems, events are generated by devices and sensors, and the EDA pattern can be used to manage the flow of these events and process them in real-time.
- **Financial systems**: EDA can handle high-volume transactions and manage real-time updates to account balances and other financial data.
- **E-commerce**: In e-commerce systems, events such as product purchases or customer updates can trigger a series of actions, such as updating inventory levels, sending notifications, and generating reports. EDA can be used to manage these events and ensure that the system can respond to them in real-time.
- **Gaming**: In gaming systems, player movements or in-game actions can trigger updates to the game state or the user interface. EDA can be used to manage these events and ensure that the system can respond to them in real-time.

Generally, EDA can be used in any system where events are a critical architecture component and real-time processing is required. Using EDA, systems can be designed to be more flexible, scalable, and responsive, and handled better with the flow of events in real-time.

Event-driven architecture example

Below is an illustration of how an e-commerce website can employ an event-driven architecture. This design pattern enables the e-commerce site to quickly respond to changes from multiple sources, even during the peak demand, without compromising system stability or excessive resource allocation.

Refer to the following figure:

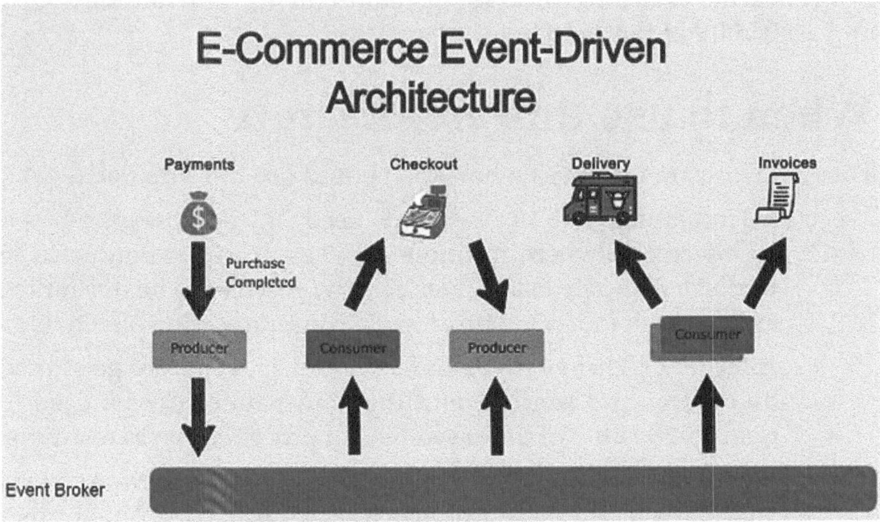

***Figure 1.2**: Implementing EDA in E-Commerce*

When customers are ready to complete their online purchase, they input their payment information on the e-commerce platform. This action of submitting the payment information generates the payment submitted event, along with the credit card information. The event router, based on the event's metadata, then directs the notification of this event to the payment service.

Upon receiving the notification, the payment service processes the event and creates a new payment processed event indicating the outcome of the operation, whether it be success or failure.

The event router then returns the updated information to the **User Interface (UI)**, displaying the customer's status and prompting them to take certain actions. For instance, if the payment fails, the UI will reopen the form to correct details. However, if the payment is successful, the UI will display the final order information and estimated delivery date.

It is worth noting that neither the front-end site nor the back-end services know each other's existence, and they simply subscribe to the **Payment Submitted** and **Payment Processed** events, which the event router manages.

Advantages of EDA

Event-driven architecture demonstrates leveraging this pattern to create flexible systems responding to event changes. EDA identifies, processes, and reacts to events. It continuously examines and assesses how events happen, change, and develop within your business operations in real-time, allowing quicker and more effective decisions.

Loosely coupled

Loose coupling is a design principle that refers to decoupling components or systems from each other, so that they can evolve and change independently. In EDA, loose coupling separates the event generation and event processing components.

In EDA, services communicate with each other through events, instead of direct calls or requests. An event broker, such as a message queue, handles the distribution of events to the appropriate services. The services do not have to be aware of the existence of each other and can be developed, tested, and deployed independently.

This loose coupling makes the system more flexible, scalable, and resilient. If one service fails, it does not necessarily affect other services, and the system can continue to operate. Additionally, services can be updated or replaced without affecting the other parts of the system, allowing for continuous development and improvement.

In short, loose coupling in EDA allows for greater flexibility, scalability, and resilience in the system, and enables services to evolve and change independently.

Immutability

In EDA immutability refers to the idea that events, once created, should not be changed. This means that events should be read-only, with their content preserved in their original form.

In EDA, events are used to communicate between services and record what has happened in the system. If events were allowed to be modified after they were created, this could lead to inconsistencies and introduce errors into the system.

By making events immutable, EDA can ensure the reliability and integrity of the data passed between services. It also enables the creation of a complete and accurate history of the events in the system, which can be used for auditing and debugging purposes.

Additionally, immutability in EDA makes implementing a scalable and resilient system easier. Events can be stored in a message queue, allowing processing to occur asynchronously and in parallel. If a service fails, the events can be replayed, ensuring that no events are lost and the system can continue operating.

In conclusion, immutability in event-driven architecture is a key aspect that ensures the reliability and accuracy of the data passed between services and creates a scalable and resilient system.

Fault tolerance

Fault tolerance refers to the ability of a system to continue operating even in the presence of failures or errors. In EDA fault tolerance is an important aspect, as it helps to ensure that the system can continue to operate even if one or more services fail.

In EDA, events are used to communicate between services, and a message queue is used to manage the distribution of events. The message queue acts as a buffer, allowing asynchronous processing of events, and ensuring that events are not lost even if a service fails. The message queue also allows the events to be replayed if necessary, ensuring the system can continue operating despite failures.

Additionally, EDA enables the creation of multiple service instances, known as a service instance. This allows for load balancing and redundancy so that if one service instance fails, another can take its place.

Overall, using events, message queues, and multiple service instances in EDA helps ensure that the system can continue operating despite failures or errors. This provides high fault tolerance, critical for mission-critical systems and applications.

Real-time

Real-time refers to a system's ability to respond and process events as they occur, without significant delay. In EDA real-time processing is a key aspect, enabling systems and applications to respond quickly to events and make decisions based on up-to-date information.

In EDA, events are used to communicate between services and record what has happened in the system. Using a message queue, events can be processed as soon as they occur, allowing for real-time analysis and decision making. The message queue also enables asynchronous processing, so that events can be processed in parallel, without blocking other system parts.

This real-time processing capability is particularly important in applications where time-sensitive information is critical, such as in financial trading, transportation, or security systems. By providing real-time information, EDA enables organizations to make informed decisions quickly and react to changing situations promptly.

Overall, real-time processing is a key aspect of event-driven architecture, enabling systems and applications to respond quickly to events and make decisions based on up-to-date information. This is critical in applications where time-sensitive information is important.

Scalability

Scalability refers to the ability of a system to handle an increasing amount of work, users, or data, without degradation of performance. In EDA, scalability is key, enabling systems and applications to grow and adapt to changing demands.

In EDA, events are used to communicate between services, and a message queue is used to manage the distribution of events. The message queue acts as a buffer, allowing for asynchronous processing of events, which helps to ensure that the system can continue to operate even if one or more services fail. The message queue also enables load balancing, so that events can be distributed across multiple service instances, helping to ensure that the system can scale to meet increasing demands.

Additionally, EDA enables the creation of microservices, which are small, independent services that can be deployed and scaled independently. This allows for more granular control over the system, enabling individual services to be scaled as needed, without affecting the rest of the system.

Overall, using events, message queues, and microservices in EDA helps the system scale to meet increasing demands. This is critical for applications that need to handle large amounts of data or large numbers of users, and for organizations that need to adapt to changing business needs.

Recovery

Recovery refers to the ability of a system to return to normal operation after a failure. In EDA, recovery is a key aspect, as it ensures that the system can continue to operate even in the event of failure.

In EDA, events are used to communicate between services, and a message queue is used to manage the distribution of events. The message queue acts as a buffer, allowing for asynchronous processing of events, which helps to ensure that the system can continue to operate even if one or more services fail. The message queue also enables load balancing, so that events can be distributed across multiple service instances, helping to ensure that the system can continue to operate even if one or more instances fail.

Additionally, EDA enables the creation of microservices, which are small, independent services that can be deployed and scaled independently. This allows for more granular control over the system, enabling individual services to be restarted or replaced as needed, without affecting the rest of the system.

Overall, using events, message queues, and microservices in EDA helps ensure that the system can continue operating even in the event of failure. This is critical for applications that must maintain availability and organizations that must ensure business continuity in the face of failures or other disruptions.

Asynchronous processing

Asynchronous processing refers to the ability of a system to process events or tasks without waiting for a response from other parts of the system. In EDA, asynchronous processing is a key aspect. It enables systems and applications to respond to events and execute tasks efficiently, without being blocked or slowed down by other system parts.

In EDA, events are used to communicate between services, and a message queue is used to manage the distribution of events. The message queue acts as a buffer, allowing for asynchronous processing of events, so services can process and respond to them as they become available, without waiting for other system parts to complete their tasks.

This helps to ensure that the system can continue to operate even if one or more services fail, as events can be rerouted and processed by other parts of the system. Additionally, asynchronous processing helps ensure the system can respond to events and execute tasks quickly, even in the face of large amounts of data or high numbers of users.

Overall, asynchronous processing is a key aspect of EDA, helping to ensure that the system can respond to events and execute tasks efficiently and effectively, without being blocked or slowed down by other parts of the system. This is critical for applications that need to handle large amounts of data or high numbers of users, and for organizations that need to respond quickly to changing business needs.

Flexibility

Flexibility refers to the ability of a system to adapt to changing requirements and conditions. In **event-driven architecture (EDA)**, flexibility is a key aspect, as it enables systems and applications to respond to real-time changes without requiring extensive modifications or redesigns.

In EDA, events are used to communicate between services, and a message queue is used to manage the distribution of events. Events and message queues enable loosely coupled services, which can be developed, deployed, and scaled independently. This allows for more granular control over the system, enabling individual services to be modified or replaced without affecting the rest.

Additionally, using microservices in EDA enables services to be developed and deployed modularly, allowing for more flexible and scalable systems. Microservices can be created, tested, and deployed independently, making adding new functionality or modifying existing services easier.

Using events, message queues, and microservices in EDA enables systems and applications to respond to changes quickly and easily, without requiring extensive modifications or redesigns. This is critical for organizations that respond quickly to business needs and systems that adapt to changing conditions in real time.

Challenges of EDA

Event-driven architecture is a modern approach to building and operating software systems, but like any architecture, it presents some challenges that organizations need to consider and address. Some of the challenges of EDA include:

Complexity

One of the biggest challenges of EDA is its complexity. EDA involves many loosely coupled services, making designing, implementing, and managing more challenging than traditional monolithic architectures. Each service must be designed and implemented to respond to specific events, which requires a deep understanding of the event structure and behavior. In addition, the coordination and integration of services can be complex, requiring robust event management and messaging systems to ensure that events are distributed and processed correctly.

Debugging and testing

Debugging and testing can present a significant challenge in EDA. Unlike traditional monolithic architectures where all components are tightly integrated and can be tested together, EDA involves multiple loosely coupled services, each with unique events and message queues. This decentralized and fragmented nature of EDA requires a different approach to testing and debugging, which can be time-consuming and challenging.

To thoroughly test and debug an EDA system, each service must be tested and debugged separately, and in combination with other services. This can involve testing each service's ability to respond to specific events and to process events in the correct order. The message queues must also be tested to ensure they can handle the volume and frequency of events and route them to the correct services.

In EDA, the events must be thoroughly tested, as they play a critical role in determining the system's behavior. The events must be properly structured and formatted and generated and processed in the correct sequence.

Given the decentralized and fragmented nature of EDA, debugging and testing can be a complex and time-consuming process that requires a strong understanding of the architecture and a well-planned approach. Nevertheless, it is an essential part of ensuring the reliability and performance of the system in production.

Event management

EDA relies heavily on a robust event management system to handle the high volume and velocity of events generated in real-time. The system must be capable of effectively processing, distributing, and storing the generated events and scale and adapt to changing conditions, such as increased event volume and velocity. The event management system is a critical component of EDA, as it serves as the backbone that supports the entire event-driven system.

Moreover, the event management system must be secure and reliable, as events may contain sensitive information that must be protected. In an EDA system, the event management system acts as a bridge between various services, enabling communication and collaboration. Hence, investing in a robust and secure event management system is important to ensure an EDA implementation's success. The system must be able to handle the vast amounts of data generated in real-time, while also ensuring the confidentiality and privacy of the information. A strong event management system is essential to ensure that events are processed and distributed in a timely and accurate manner and that the system operates efficiently and effectively.

Scalability

Scalability is a crucial aspect of EDA, as the system must adapt to growth in real-time. As the system grows and generates more data and events, the architecture must handle the increased volume and velocity of events without compromising performance, reliability, and maintainability. This requires a scalable event-driven architecture that can handle large amounts of real-time data and events while ensuring the system remains stable and manageable.

To achieve scalability in EDA, it is necessary to implement robust event management and messaging systems, use scalable storage and computing resources, and optimize the processing and distribution of events. In addition, it is important to continuously monitor and evaluate the system's performance and make necessary adjustments to ensure that the system remains scalable and responsive to the changing needs of the business.

Data management

EDA requires a data management system that is highly efficient, flexible, and secure. This system must be able to handle the variety of data formats generated by different events, and it must be able to process data in real-time, regardless of the volume and velocity of events. In addition, the data management system must be secure, as it will often contain sensitive information that must be protected.

The system must also be scalable, able to handle increasing amounts of data as the system grows. This requires careful planning, design, and modern data management technologies like NoSQL databases, data lakes, and data streaming platforms. The data management system must also be integrated with the event management system, allowing for seamless processing and distribution of events and data.

Security

EDA involves the flow of sensitive information between various microservices, making data security a crucial aspect of the architecture. This necessitates the implementation of a secure and dependable security infrastructure that can protect sensitive information from any unauthorized access, tampering or theft.

The security infrastructure must be thoughtfully crafted to guarantee the confidentiality, accuracy, and accessibility of the data being exchanged between services. It must handle an increased demand for security as the system grows, without affecting the performance or reliability of the overall architecture. To ensure the proper functioning of EDA, it is vital to implement robust security measures that can mitigate potential security threats and prevent data breaches, as protecting sensitive information is of utmost importance.

Latency

EDA relies on processing events in real-time to achieve its intended outcomes. This requirement can result in several latency issues that can impact the performance and reliability of the system. Latency refers to the delay between the generation of an event and its processing, which can occur for various reasons. For example, events may be generated faster than they can be processed, resulting in a backlog of unprocessed events. Alternatively, services may take too long to process events, resulting in increased latency.

These latency issues can significantly impact the accuracy and consistency of the systems that rely on the EDA. For example, if events are generated faster than they can be processed, some events may be lost or ignored, leading to data inconsistencies and inaccuracies. Additionally, if services take too long to process events, the data they rely on may be outdated or incorrect, resulting in inaccurate results.

To address these latency issues, it is essential to have an infrastructure in place that can process events as quickly as possible, while ensuring the accuracy and consistency of the data. This may involve optimizing the processing algorithms services use, increasing the number of parallel processing threads, or using more powerful hardware to handle the increased processing demands. It may also involve investing in real-time analytics tools and techniques to monitor the system's performance and identify potential bottlenecks in real-time.

Monitoring and maintenance

Event-driven architecture (EDA) is a complex and dynamic system that involves many different components, including services, events, and message queues. Each component plays a critical role in the system's operation and must work together seamlessly and efficiently to deliver the desired outcomes. This complexity can make monitoring and maintaining the EDA system challenging to ensure it always operates optimally.

To address this challenge, it is essential to have a robust monitoring and maintenance infrastructure in place. This infrastructure should be designed to detect and resolve issues in real-time so that any potential problems are addressed quickly and effectively before they have a chance to impact the system's overall performance. Additionally, this infrastructure should be scalable to handle increased demand as the system grows and evolves.

A robust monitoring and maintenance infrastructure helps ensure that the EDA system operates efficiently and effectively, delivering the desired outcomes for your business. Designing and implementing such an infrastructure requires significant time, resources, and expertise. Still, its benefits in improved system performance and reduced downtime are worth the investment.

Evolving events

As technology and businesses continuously evolve, systems and applications must adapt. One crucial aspect of this adaptation is managing and updating events within an EDA. As the system develops over time, events must be updated to reflect its new characteristics, which can be a complex and challenging. The challenge arises when trying to update events without affecting other microservices within the system. This can be especially difficult in a distributed scenario where different teams are responsible for creating and processing events. In such situations, ensuring that the updates made to events are coordinated and consistent can be challenging, without impacting the operation of other microservices that rely on these events. Here event consumers are not in direct contact with event producers, it poses an additional challenge to maintain a smooth and effective processing of events. This is because misinterpretations or miscommunications can result in unintended outcomes. Hence, managing the evolving events within an EDA requires careful planning and coordination to ensure that updates are made smoothly, without disrupting the system's operation.

Overall, while EDA can bring many benefits to organizations, it also presents some challenges that must be addressed. These challenges require careful planning, design, implementation, and ongoing monitoring and maintenance to ensure that EDA systems and applications operate efficiently, effectively, and securely.

Comparing EDA with other architectural patterns

EDA is a relatively new architectural pattern that has emerged with the growth of microservices and cloud-based systems. Unlike traditional monolithic architecture, EDA is a distributed and loosely coupled architecture that relies on exchanging events between services. Other common architectural patterns include:

Monolithic architecture

Monolithic architecture is a software development approach that structures an application as a single, self-contained unit, in which all the components of the application are tightly coupled and run together as a single executable codebase. This means the entire application is deployed as a single package and runs on a single server or cluster of servers.

The application is typically developed as a single codebase in a monolithic architecture. All the application's components, including the user interface, business logic, and data storage, are integrated into a single executable file. This architecture style has been around for many years and was the dominant approach in software development until the rise of cloud computing and microservices architecture.

Monolithic architecture has some advantages, including its simplicity, ease of development, testing, and the ability to handle many users and requests. It can also be easier to deploy, monitor, and maintain since all the application components are in a single package. However, as the application grows and complexity, monolithic architecture can become less scalable, flexible, and maintainable.

One of the main disadvantages of monolithic architecture is that all the application components are tightly coupled, making it difficult to change or update the application. This can lead to long release cycles, as changes to one component can affect the entire application, requiring extensive testing and validation. In addition, the architecture may not be suitable for large-scale applications with a high degree of complexity, as it can become difficult to manage and maintain.

Another disadvantage of monolithic architecture is that it can be challenging to scale the application horizontally. Adding more resources to the application may not improve performance, as the entire application must be scaled together. This can lead to overprovisioning resources, which can be costly and inefficient.

While monolithic architecture is a straightforward approach to software development, it can have limitations as applications grow and complexity. For this reason, many organizations have begun to adopt microservices architecture or other distributed architectural patterns to address these challenges.

Microservices architecture

Microservices architecture is a software architecture pattern in which a large application is broken down into multiple small, independent, and autonomous services. Each microservice is designed to perform a specific business function and communicates with other microservices via well-defined APIs. The microservices are loosely coupled, so they can be developed, deployed, and scaled independently, allowing for greater agility, flexibility, and resilience than traditional monolithic architectures.

Each microservice runs as a separate process in microservices architecture and can be developed using different technologies and programming languages. This allows development teams to use the most appropriate tools for each microservice, which can result in faster development and better-quality code. Each microservice can also be developed and deployed separately, which allows for more frequent releases and faster time-to-market.

To ensure that the microservices can communicate with each other effectively, they use APIs and protocols that are well-defined and easily understood.

Microservices architecture also allows for better fault tolerance and scalability. If one microservice fails, it does not bring down the entire system, and the other microservices can continue to function and serve requests. Scaling can also be done at a microservice level, which allows for more precise scaling and better resource utilization.

Overall, microservices architecture is a flexible, scalable, and resilient approach to software development that can help organizations achieve faster time-to-market, better quality software, and more efficient use of resources. However, it does require careful planning, design, and implementation to ensure that the microservices are properly decoupled and that the communication between them is effective and efficient.

Service-Oriented Architecture

Service-Oriented Architecture (SOA) is a software architectural pattern that designs loosely coupled and distributed services that can be reused and combined to create larger applications. The SOA approach emphasizes creating modular services that can be accessed and invoked over a network through standard communication protocols.

In a service-oriented architecture, services are the fundamental building blocks of the system, and they are designed to be self-contained, independent, and interoperable. Services can be developed, deployed, and maintained independently and can be composed to create higher-level business processes or applications.

SOA services are typically accessed through web services or APIs, which provide a standardized way of accessing the service and its data. Standardized interfaces allow services to be easily combined with other services to create more complex applications. This modular and interoperable approach promotes reusability and flexibility, allowing for changes to be made to one service without affecting other services in the system.

SOA systems are often built using middleware, which provides a layer of abstraction between the services and the underlying operating system, network, and hardware. This middleware can provide additional functionality such as security, messaging, and orchestration of service interactions.

One of the key benefits of SOA is that it allows organizations to break down large monolithic applications into smaller and manageable services. This approach can help reduce development costs, increase flexibility, and improve the ability to adapt to changing business requirements.

However, implementing a SOA can also present challenges. One of the main challenges is ensuring that services are designed with appropriate granularity and are sufficiently decoupled from one another. In addition, ensuring that the services are highly available, reliable, and secure can require careful planning and implementation.

Model-View-Controller architecture

The **Model-View-Controller** (**MVC**) architecture is a software design pattern that separates an application into three interconnected components: the model, the view, and the controller. This pattern is widely used to develop user interfaces, particularly web applications.

The model represents the data and the business logic of the application. It is responsible for managing the data and providing the necessary functionality to access and manipulate it. The model provides an interface that allows the controller and the view to access and modify the data but does not interact with them directly.

The view is responsible for presenting the data to the user. It represents the user interface and displays the information provided by the model. The view interacts with the user and receives input but does not modify the data directly. The view sends the user input to the controller, updating the model accordingly.

The controller is responsible for handling the user input and updating the model and the view accordingly. It receives input from the user through the view and processes it by interacting with the model. Once the model is updated, the controller updates the view to reflect the changes made to the data.

The MVC architecture promotes the separation of concerns, which makes the application more maintainable and easier to modify. It also allows for parallel development of the components, leading to faster development and easier collaboration between developers. Moreover, the MVC architecture can improve the application's testability, as each component can be tested independently.

Overall, the MVC architecture is a widely used software design pattern that separates an application into three interconnected components, providing a well-organized and maintainable structure for developing user interfaces.

Key components of EDA

EDA relies on key components that work together seamlessly to enable real-time event processing and streamlined data flow. Let us explore these components in more detail to understand how they form the foundation of an effective EDA.

Event emitter

In an event-driven system, an event emitter is a component that generates events and emits them to the rest of the system. An event emitter could be any software module, hardware device, user interface element, or external system that can detect and report some action or state change.

An event emitter generates events by executing a specific code path that represents the occurrence of a particular action or state change. For example, a button on a user interface could be an event emitter that generates an event when clicked. The event emitter runs a code path when the button is pressed to create an event object, fill it with pertinent information, and emit it to the rest of the system.

The event object generated by an event emitter typically includes a name, a set of properties, and an optional payload. The name identifies the type of event, such as **buttonClicked** or **temperatureChanged**.

The properties provide additional information about the event, such as the timestamp, the source of the event, or any relevant context. The payload, if present, contains additional data specific to the event and needed by the event consumers.

After generating the event object, the emitter typically emits the event to the event bus or directly to interested consumers. The emitter does not directly handle the event or its processing but generates and emits it to other components.

In an event-driven system, emitters provide a flexible and responsive architecture. By generating events, they allow other system components to respond to the changes in the system's state and trigger appropriate actions. Event emitters can be decoupled from the rest of the system, allowing for easier maintenance, testing, and scalability. They also allow for event-driven architectures that handle asynchronous, real-time, or distributed scenarios.

Event listeners

In an event-driven system, an event listener is a component that listens for and handles events emitted by event emitters. Event listeners typically subscribe to specific events on the event bus and perform certain actions in response to those events.

When an event is emitted, the bus routes it to all registered event listeners interested. The event listeners then execute their specific code path that handles the event. The code path may include updating a database, triggering another event, sending a notification, or updating a user interface.

Event listeners are typically decoupled from event emitters and other system components. They do not know or care about the specific source of the event, but only respond to events that match their subscription criteria. This allows for a loosely-coupled, scalable, and flexible architecture, where components can be added, removed, or replaced without affecting the overall system behavior.

Event listeners can also be designed to handle events in various ways, depending on the system's specific requirements. For example, an event listener could execute its handling code in a separate thread or process to improve performance or prioritize events based on their type or source. Event listeners can also be designed to handle errors or exceptions during event processing, ensuring that the system remains resilient and responsive.

In summary, event listeners are a crucial component of event-driven systems. They allow other components to respond to system state changes and trigger appropriate actions. They provide a flexible, responsive architecture that handles asynchronous, real-time, or distributed scenarios. They also allow for decoupling, scalability, and easy system maintenance.

Event bus

In an event-driven architecture, an event bus is a communication channel or message broker that enables emitters to publish events and event listeners to subscribe to and consume events. The event bus mediates between emitters and listeners, allowing them to communicate decoupled and asynchronously.

The event bus provides a central point for all events in the system and ensures that events are reliably delivered to interested listeners. It also provides various features such as filtering, routing, and prioritization of events, to enable more fine-grained control over the event flow.

When an event emitter emits an event, it is sent to the event bus with a specific event name and payload. The event bus then delivers the event to all registered listeners who subscribe to the event name. The event listeners can perform specific actions in response to the event, such as updating a database, triggering another event, or updating a user interface.

Event buses can be designed to handle different types of events and use various messaging protocols, such as publish-subscribe, request-response, or point-to-point. They can also be implemented using message queues, message brokers, or in-memory systems.

The event bus enables loose coupling, scalability, and system flexibility in an event-driven architecture. Decoupling event emitters and listeners allows for easier system maintenance, testing, and extension. It also enables the system to handle real-time, asynchronous, and distributed scenarios, by providing a reliable and efficient communication channel for events.

Event processing

Event processing is the rules and logic governing how the system handles events in an EDA. Event processing involves receiving events from event emitters, performing necessary manipulations or transformations on the event data, and routing the events to the appropriate listeners.

Depending on the system's requirements, event processing can involve various operations. Some common types of event processing include:

- **Filtering**: This involves selecting a subset of events that meet specific criteria, such as event type, source, or data content. Filtering can help reduce the amount of data that needs to be processed and improve the system's performance.
- Aggregation involves combining multiple events into a single event or data structure. Aggregation can help simplify event processing and reduce the complexity of the system.
- **Enrichment**: This involves adding additional data to events to provide context or to enable more detailed analysis. Enrichment can include data from external sources, such as APIs or databases, or other events within the system.
- **Routing**: This involves determining the appropriate event listeners to receive each event. Routing can be based on various factors, such as event type, event data, or the location or status of the event listeners.
- Transformation involves changing the structure or format of events to make them compatible with the requirements of the event listeners or other systems. Transformation can involve converting data types, encoding formats, or data structures.

Overall, event processing is a critical component of EDA, as it enables the system to manage and respond to events in a flexible and scalable way. By performing various operations on events, event processing ensures that event data is accurate, relevant, and promptly delivered to the appropriate listeners.

Common use cases for EDA

Let us explore some common use cases for EDA to understand its practical applications and benefits better.

Banking system

EDA has numerous use cases in banking systems, including enabling real-time processing of financial transactions and enhancing the customer experience. Some of the common use case in banking are given below:

- **Real-time transaction processing**: EDA can facilitate the processing of financial transactions in real time, allowing account balances to be updated immediately when a customer deposits or withdrawals. This ensures that customers have accurate and up-to-date information about their finances.
- **Fraud detection**: EDA can detect fraudulent activity in banking systems by triggering alerts for unusual account activity, multiple failed login attempts, or transactions that exceed a certain limit. This can help banks identify and prevent fraudulent transactions in real-time.
- **Customer service**: EDA can improve the customer service experience in banking systems by enabling real-time notifications to customer service representatives when customers make account inquiries or request new services. This allows banks to provide faster and more personalized customer service.
- **Risk management**: EDA can manage risks in banking systems by triggering alerts for events such as changes in interest rates, market fluctuations, or geopolitical events. This helps banks identify and mitigate risks in real-time, reducing the likelihood of financial losses.
- **Compliance**: EDA can help banks ensure compliance with regulatory requirements by triggering alerts for regulation changes or audit findings. This enables banks to stay up-to-date with regulatory requirements and avoid penalties for non-compliance.

Media streaming platform

Media streaming platforms, such as YouTube, Netflix, and Amazon Prime Video, rely heavily on EDA to deliver their users high-quality, reliable, and scalable streaming services. Here are some use cases for EDA in media streaming platforms:

- **Content ingestion**: Media streaming platforms must ingest a large amount of content from various sources, such as studios, broadcasters, and content creators. EDA handles this process by generating events when new content is added to the platform. These events are propagated to various services that process the content and make it available for streaming.

- **User authentication**: When a user logs in to a media streaming platform, an event is generated and propagated to various services to authenticate the user. This process ensures that the user has the appropriate permissions to access the content and services offered by the platform.
- **Content delivery**: EDA is used to manage content delivery to users. When a user requests a video, an event is generated and propagated to various services to route the request to the appropriate server. This ensures the content is delivered efficiently and reliably to the user's device.
- **Playback**: EDA handles the playback process by generating events when users click the "play" button. These events are propagated to various services that stream the content to the user's device.
- **Personalization**: Media streaming platforms use EDA to personalize the user experience by analyzing user behavior and preferences. When users interact with the platform, events are generated and processed to provide personalized recommendations and suggestions.
- **Performance monitoring**: EDA monitors the performance of media streaming platforms. Events are generated when errors or issues occur, which are used to troubleshoot and diagnose problems.

Supply chain management

EDA is becoming increasingly popular in **Supply chain management (SCM)** as it provides a flexible and scalable approach to managing complex, interconnected systems. Here are some use cases for EDA in SCM:

- **Inventory management**: EDA manages inventory levels by generating events when inventory levels reach a certain threshold. These events are propagated to various services that trigger reorder requests, ensuring that inventory levels are maintained optimally.
- **Order management**: EDA manages the order fulfillment process by generating events when an order is placed. These events are propagated to various services that process the order, including picking, packing, and shipping.

- **Tracking and tracing**: EDA tracks and traces products through the supply chain. Events are generated when products are scanned or moved, which are used to update the product's status in real-time.
- **Demand forecasting**: EDA forecasts demand by generating events when customer behavior changes. These events are propagated to various services that analyze the data and adjust production schedules and inventory levels accordingly.
- **Supply chain optimization**: EDA optimizes the supply chain by generating events when delays or disruptions occur. These events are used to reroute products or adjust schedules to minimize the impact on the supply chain.
- **Supplier management**: EDA manages suppliers by generating events when supplier performance falls below acceptable levels. These events are propagated to various services that trigger corrective actions, such as renegotiating contracts or finding new suppliers.

Popular technologies and frameworks used in EDA

Some popular technologies and frameworks used in EDA are:

RabbitMQ

RabbitMQ is an open-source message broker software that enables applications to communicate with each other by exchanging messages. It is a popular implementation of the **Advanced Message Queuing Protocol (AMQP)** and can be used as middleware to decouple applications and services.

RabbitMQ works by receiving messages from producers and then routing them to consumers based on certain rules or patterns. Producers are applications or services that generate messages and send them to RabbitMQ for delivery, while consumers are applications or services that receive messages from RabbitMQ.

In RabbitMQ, messages are sent to an exchange, which then routes them to one or more queues based on certain routing rules. Queues hold messages until a consumer consumes them, and consumers can retrieve messages from queues in a **First-in, First-out** (**FIFO**) order or based on certain priority rules.

RabbitMQ provides various messaging patterns such as publish/subscribe, request/reply, and point-to-point messaging. It also supports features such as message acknowledgments, message persistence, and message routing.

RabbitMQ is widely used in microservices architectures, enabling services to communicate asynchronously and decouples them from each other. It is also used in event-driven architectures, facilitating event streaming and event-driven processing.

Overall, RabbitMQ is a reliable and flexible message broker that enables applications and services to communicate with each other in a decoupled and scalable way.

Apache Kafka

Apache Kafka is an open source distributed streaming platform originally developed at LinkedIn. It is designed to handle large volumes of real-time data from various sources and enables organizations to build scalable, fault-tolerant, event-driven architectures.

At a high level, Kafka works by receiving data in the form of messages from producers and then storing them in a distributed cluster of servers called brokers. Consumers can then read the messages from the brokers and process them as needed. Kafka provides various messaging patterns such as publish/subscribe, request/reply, and point-to-point messaging.

Kafka is built around the concept of topics, which are logical categories or streams of messages. Producers send messages to a topic; consumers can read messages from one or more topics. Kafka provides high flexibility regarding message retention and delivery guarantees, enabling organizations to configure Kafka to meet their specific requirements.

It also provides several features to ensure fault-tolerance and high availability. It also supports partitioning and re-balancing, enabling Kafka to scale to handle large volumes of data.

Kafka is widely used in various industries such as finance, e-commerce, and social media to handle real-time transactional data, logs, and sensor data. It is also commonly used in microservices and event-driven architectures to facilitate event streaming, data ingestion, and data processing.

Overall, Kafka is a powerful and scalable streaming platform that enables organizations to build real-time event-driven architectures that can handle large volumes of data and respond quickly to changing conditions.

AWS Lambda

In an EDA, AWS Lambda can execute functions or processes in response to events generated by other services or applications. Lambda can be used as a **Function-as-a-service** (**FaaS**) provider to execute code in response to an event, and then return the result to the calling service.

For example, suppose an application generates an event such as a new customer registration or a product sale. In that case, the event can be sent to an AWS service such as Amazon **Simple Notification Service** (**SNS**) or Amazon **Simple Queue Service** (**SQS**). The event can then trigger an AWS Lambda function that performs a specific action, such as sending a confirmation email to the customer, updating the product inventory, or performing analytics on the event data.

AWS Lambda provides a highly scalable and cost-effective solution for processing event-driven workloads in an EDA. With Lambda, developers can write functions that are triggered in response to specific events, and then scale these functions automatically to handle high volumes of event traffic. Lambda functions are stateless, which means they can be executed concurrently and in parallel, enabling high throughput and low latency.

Lambda functions can also be used with AWS services such as Amazon DynamoDB, Amazon Kinesis, and Amazon S3 to build real-time, event-driven applications. For example, Lambda can process data from a Kinesis data stream in real-time, performing real-time analytics on the data and triggering other events based on the analysis results.

AWS Lambda provides a powerful and flexible solution for implementing event-driven architectures in the cloud. It enables organizations to build scalable, cost-effective, highly responsive applications that quickly and easily respond to changing business requirements.

Azure event grid

Azure event grid is a serverless event routing service provided by Microsoft Azure that enables developers to build event-driven architectures in the cloud. It provides a flexible and scalable infrastructure for routing events between different services and applications.

An EDA azure event grid can capture and route events from various sources to different targets. Developers can define event publishers and subscribers, and then configure event grid to route events based on specific criteria.

For example, if an application generates an event such as a new customer registration or a product sale, the event can be sent to event grid. The event grid can then route the event to an Azure function, Logic App, or other service designed to process the event. The processing can include updating a database, sending notifications, or triggering other events.

Azure event grid supports a variety of event sources, including Azure services such as Blob Storage, Event Hubs, and IoT Hub, as well as custom events from applications and third-party services. It also supports a variety of event handlers, including Azure Functions, Logic Apps, and Webhooks.

Event grid provides several features that makes it easy to build event-driven architectures. These include advanced filtering capabilities, which enable developers to specify which events should be routed to specific targets, and retry policies, ensuring that events are processed even during temporary failures.

These technologies and frameworks enable developers to design and implement robust event-driven architectures that can handle high volumes of real-time events and respond quickly to changing conditions.

Conclusion

In this chapter, we learned **event-driven architecture (EDA)** focuses on events as the primary building blocks of the system, with communication through an event bus or message queue. It offers scalability, flexibility, and modularity, making it suitable for quickly handling large amounts of data. However, EDA can also present challenges like increased complexity and latency. EDA stands out in decoupling and asynchronous communication compared to other architectural patterns.

The key components of EDA include event producers, topics, event consumers, event bus, loose coupling, event-based communication, event ordering, idempotence, event schema, event sourcing, and CQRS. EDA is commonly used in various applications, including financial services, e-commerce, IoT, and real-time monitoring systems.

We also learned that popular technologies and frameworks used in EDA include Apache Kafka, RabbitMQ, AWS Lambda, and Azure Event Hubs. EDA allows developers to build systems that can handle a high volume of events and respond to them in real-time, making it ideal for complex systems that process large amounts of data. EDA offers greater flexibility and scalability than traditional software architecture and can be used to build highly distributed systems. Overall, EDA is an effective architectural pattern for building complex, scalable, and distributed systems that can handle large volumes of data, making it a popular choice for modern software development.

In the next chapter, you will explore the basic concepts and principles that serve as the foundation of event-driven architecture. Gaining a deep understanding of these concepts is crucial for creating systems that depend on event-driven architecture. Thus, it is important to grasp these concepts thoroughly to develop successful event-driven systems.

CHAPTER 2
Core Concepts of Event-Driven Architecture

Introduction

Event-driven architecture is a way to design software where events are the focus and different parts of the system communicate through an event bus or message queue. It is used in applications that need quick processing and the ability to handle a lot of users or data simultaneously, where different parts of the system do not have to depend on each other.

Structure

This chapter will cover the following topics:

- Event producers
- Topics
- Event consumers
- Event bus
- Loose coupling
- Event-based communication
- Event ordering and idempotence

- Event schema
- Event sourcing
- Command Query Responsibility Segregation

Objectives

This chapter comprehensively explains the key concepts and principles of **event-driven architecture** (EDA), including event producers, event consumers, event buses, etc. It will help developers and architects understand the core components of EDA and how event-driven architecture fits into the larger landscape of modern application development, including cloud-native and microservices architectures.

Event producers

In an event-driven architecture, an event producer is a crucial component that generates event messages in response to specific actions or conditions. These messages typically contain data or metadata that provide details about the action or condition that triggered the event. Once generated, these events are sent to an event bus or broker to be consumed by other components or systems.

The role of event producers

The primary responsibility of an event producer is to serve as the primary source of truth for events in the event-driven system. This involves ensuring that events are generated accurately, contain reliable information, and promptly publish them to the event bus. The overall success of an event-driven system depends on the quality of events produced by the event producer.

Event producer metadata is extra information an event producer includes with an event message in an event-driven architecture. This metadata gives downstream components or systems important details about the event's source, generation time, and other relevant information to interpret and process the event effectively.

For example, an event producer might include metadata in an event message that describes the event type, the schema's version, a unique identifier for the event, the user who triggered the event, and any relevant data associated with the event. This metadata provides additional context about the event, such as the source of the event, the time it was generated, and any other relevant details that can help downstream components or systems interpret and process the event correctly.

The following is an example of event producer metadata that might be included in an event producer message:


```
{
"eventType": "purchase",
"timestamp": "2023-03-04T10:15:00Z",
"eventSource": "ecommerce_website",
"eventVersion": "1.0",
"eventID": "123456789",
"userID": "johndoe123",
"totalAmount": 49.99,
"items": [
 {
"sku": "ABC123",
"name": "Product 1",
"quantity": 2,
"price": 24.99
 },
            {
"sku": "XYZ789",
"name": "Product 2",
"quantity": 1,
"price": 24.99
              }
          ]
}
```


In the above-given example, the event producer metadata includes the following information:

- **`eventType`**: Indicates the type of event, in this case, a purchase event.
- **`timestamp`**: Indicates the time that the event was generated in ISO 8601 format.

- `eventSource`: Indicates the source of the event, in this case, an e-commerce website.
- `eventVersion`: Indicates the version of the event schema being used.
- `eventID`: Uniquely identifies the event message, which can be useful for tracing and debugging.
- `userID`: Identifies the user who made the purchase.
- `totalAmount`: Indicates the total amount of the purchase.
- `items`: Provides details about the items purchased, including the SKU, name, quantity, and price.

By including this metadata in the event message, downstream components or systems can correctly interpret and process the event and take appropriate actions based on its information. For example, a recommendation engine might use the information about the items purchased to suggest related products to the user, or a fraud detection system might use the timestamp and eventID to identify potentially fraudulent transactions.

Topics

In an event-driven architecture, a topic is a subject to which an event producer can publish events. A topic is typically a string that identifies a specific category or type of event. Event consumers can then subscribe to one or more topics to receive events of interest.

The following is an example of how topics might be used in an event-driven system for an e-commerce website:

- Topic: Purchase- Purchases-related events include orders placed, orders shipped, and orders canceled.
- Topic: Product- Events related to products, such as added, updated, and removed.
- Topic: User- Events related to users, such as user registered, user logged in, and user account deleted.

In this example, event producers would publish events related to purchases, products, and users to their respective topics. Event consumers could then selectively subscribe to topics of interest, such as subscribing to the purchase topic to receive events related to customer orders.

By using topics to organize events, event-driven systems can scale more effectively, with event consumers processing only the events that they are interested in. This allows the system to handle larger volumes of events more efficiently, improving performance and scalability.

Event consumers

Event consumers are components or systems that receive event messages generated by event producers in an event-driven system. These components or systems use the information contained in the event messages to trigger specific actions or behaviors.

Event consumers are generally responsible for processing incoming events, interpreting the data they contain, and taking the appropriate actions based on that data. This might involve updating a database, sending a notification to a user, triggering an automation process, or any other actions.

The role of event consumers

The primary role of event consumers is to consume and process event messages in a timely and efficient manner. To accomplish this, event consumers typically subscribe to one or more topics on an event bus or broker, allowing them to receive event messages relevant to their specific use case.

Once an event consumer receives an event message, it must interpret the metadata and determine what action to take based on that data. Depending on the use case, this might involve processing the data locally, sending it to a downstream system or component, or triggering a specific action within the current system or component.

A simple example of an event consumer is business logic components like systems or components that process events to trigger specific business processes or workflows. For example, an e-commerce system might have a business logic component that processes purchase events and updates the inventory database accordingly.

A simple workflow of event consumers is:

- Connect to the event bus or broker and subscribe to relevant topics.
- Wait for incoming event messages.

- When an event message is received, parse the message to extract relevant data.
- Determine the appropriate action based on the message's data.
- Execute the action, which might involve updating a database, triggering a workflow, or sending a notification.
- Log the event message and the action taken for auditing and debugging purposes.
- Continue waiting for and processing incoming event messages.
- When finished processing events, disconnect from the event bus or broker.

Processing events by event consumers:

The following is an example of the business logic that an event consumer might use to process a purchase event:

```
// Define a function to process a purchase event
function processPurchaseEvent(purchaseEventData) {

// Extract data from the Purchase event
const productID = purchaseEventData.productID;
const quantity = purchaseEventData.quantity;
const price = purchaseEventData.price;

// Update inventory database to reflect the new purchase
const inventoryItem = inventoryDatabase.
getProduct(productID);
inventoryItem.quantity -= quantity;
inventoryDatabase.saveProduct(inventoryItem);

// Update sales data to reflect the revenue generated by
the purchase
const revenue = price * quantity;
salesData.incrementRevenue(revenue);

// Trigger confirmation email to the purchaser
emailService.sendConfirmationEmail(purchaseEventData.
email, productID, quantity, price);
```

```
    // Log the event and actions taken for auditing purposes
    logger.log("Purchase event processed: " + JSON.
    stringify(purchaseEventData));

// Connect to event bus and subscribe to Purchase events
eventBus.connect();
eventBus.subscribe("Purchase");

// Loop to continuously consume events
while(true) {

    // Wait for next event message
    message = eventBus.waitForMessage();

    // Call processPurchaseEvent function to process the
    Purchase event
    processPurchaseEvent(message.data);
}}
```

Note that this is just an example. The actual business logic implemented by an event consumer may vary depending on the specific use case and the technology used for event processing. The key idea is to extract relevant data from the purchase event and use it to trigger specific actions within the system, such as updating inventory and sales data, sending confirmation emails, and logging events for auditing purposes.

Event bus

In the context of EDA, the event bus is a crucial component that serves as a middleware to connect event producers and consumers by facilitating the routing and distribution of events between them. The event bus receives events from producers and distributes them to one or more event consumers based on predefined rules. As a result, event producers do not require knowledge of the event consumers or their implementation. They send events to the event bus, which handles the rest.

The event bus decouples event producers and consumers, which allows them to operate independently of each other. This means that producers do not need to know anything about the consumers who receive their events, and consumers do not need to know anything about the producers who generate the events they receive. The event bus provides a level of abstraction between the producers and consumers, which makes the system more flexible and scalable.

Types of event buses

There are two types of event buses, which are internal and external. Internal event buses are used within a single application or service, whereas external event buses communicate between different applications or services. The choice of event bus type depends on the system's specific requirements.

Internal event bus

An internal event bus is used within a single application or service to communicate between components. The internal event bus is typically implemented as an in-memory message queue, which means that events are stored in memory and consumed by subscribers in the same process. This type of event bus is suitable for small-scale systems where performance is critical, and there is no need to communicate with external systems.

External event bus

An external event bus is used to communicate between different applications or services. The external event bus is typically implemented using a message broker such as Apache Kafka or RabbitMQ, which provides more advanced features such as persistent storage and fault tolerance. This type of event bus is suitable for large-scale systems where high availability and fault tolerance are critical.

How does the event bus work

In an EDA, events are produced by sources and consumed by handlers. Event sources are responsible for publishing events to the event bus, while handlers are responsible for subscribing to events from the event bus. The event bus receives events from event sources and then forwards them to all interested handlers.

When an event is produced, it is sent to the event bus along with any necessary metadata, such as the event type and payload. The event bus then routes the event to all event handlers subscribed to the event type. Event handlers can filter events based on metadata or content, allowing them only to process events relevant to their specific function.

Implementing an event bus can use messaging protocols such as AMQP, MQTT, HTTP, or a message broker such as RabbitMQ or Apache Kafka. The choice of protocol or broker relies on the specific system's requirements. The following is an example of how an event bus can be used in a simple online ordering system:

- A customer orders on the website, which triggers an event, and the event is sent to the event bus.
- Shipping and billing services are subscribed to the event bus and receive the event.
- The shipping service checks the order details and sends the order to the warehouse for fulfillment.
- The billing service processes the payment for the order.
- The event bus sends a confirmation event to the customer.

In this example, the event bus mediates between the order placement system and the shipping and billing services. It allows the services to operate independently of each other and asynchronously process events as they arrive. This approach allows for a more scalable, fault-tolerant, and loosely coupled architecture.

Loose coupling

Loose coupling is a crucial design principle in software engineering that seeks to minimize the interdependencies between different components or modules of a system. This principle aims to enhance the system's flexibility, maintainability, and scalability by minimizing the impact of changes in one module or other modules. By reducing the dependencies, loose coupling ensures that the system components can evolve independently without causing significant disruption to other system parts.

In an event-driven architecture, loose coupling is attained by constructing the system such that its components communicate via events. Events are messages that indicate the occurrence of an action or state change. The decoupling of components is achieved by not requiring them to know each other's internal state or implementation details. Instead, they only need a shared event bus to exchange information. This way, the components can operate independently without direct interdependence, leading to a more flexible and adaptable system.

Loose coupling in an event-driven architecture offers various advantages, such as:

- **Scalability**: Loose coupling enables easy system scalability since adding or removing components does not affect the others. This ensures the system can scale up or down to cater to changes in workload.
- **Flexibility**: Loose coupling enhances the system's flexibility by allowing modifications to be made to one component without affecting the others. This facilitates the addition of new features or the modification of existing ones.
- **Maintainability**: Loose coupling improves the system's maintainability since modifications to one component do not require changes to the others. This mitigates the risk of introducing bugs or breaking the system.
- **Reusability**: Loose coupling promotes the reusability of components since they can be used in different contexts without modification. This saves time and effort in development, making the system more cost-effective.

To achieve loose coupling in an event-driven architecture, several recommended design practices include:

- **Use a common event bus**: All components should interact through a bus, eliminating the need for direct communication.
- **Use a publish-subscribe model**: Components should publish events to the event bus, and other components should subscribe to events they are interested in. This facilitates dynamic interactions between components.
- **Use event schemas**: Events should be defined using a schema that describes their structure and content, ensuring that all components can interpret events correctly.
- **Use event-driven APIs**: Components should expose APIs based on events rather than actions, allowing for greater flexibility in their usage.

In summary, loose coupling is an essential design principle in event-driven architecture that enables systems to be more scalable, flexible, maintainable, and reusable. Components should use a common event bus, a publish-subscribe model, event schemas, and event-driven APIs to achieve loose coupling.

Event-based communication

Event-based communication is how parts of a system communicate by sending and reacting to events, which are messages that give information about something that happened. For example, a button click, or a temperature change can be an event. In this way of communicating, components do not call each other's functions directly; instead, they send and listen for events from other components.

This communication method is often used in systems where events control what happens. The different parts of the system are loosely connected and can work independently, and they use an event bus or message broker to send and receive events.

To send an event, a component creates an event object with information about what happened. The event is then sent to the event bus, which distributes it to all the components that are interested in that event.

Components that want to know about an event can subscribe to it on the event bus. When the event happens, the subscribed components receive and can react to it. The event can trigger a change in the component's behavior or a component to send out a new event, which starts a chain of events across different components.

Suppose the application consists of the following components:

- **Product catalog**: This component manages the list of available products and their details.
- **Shopping cart**: This component maintains the user's selected items and their quantities.
- **Order processing**: This component handles order placement and payment processing.

In an event-based communication model, these components interact by emitting and listening to events. Let us see how communication happens in different scenarios:

Scenario 1: User adds a product to the cart

When a user adds a product to the cart, the shopping cart component emits an event, say `ItemAddedToCart` event. The event contains the details of the added item, such as the product ID, name, and quantity. The event is then sent to the event bus, which distributes it to all subscribed components.

The product catalog component is interested in the **ItemAddedToCart** event. When the event is received, the product catalog component updates the product's availability and stock information. If the added product is out of stock, the product catalog component emits a **ProductOutOfStock** event, which the shopping cart component receives. The shopping cart component updates the user interface to show the product as out of stock and prompts the user to remove or continue shopping.

Scenario 2: User removes a product from the cart

When a user removes a product from the cart, the shopping cart component emits an **ItemRemovedFromCart** event. The event contains the details of the removed item, such as the product ID and quantity. The event is sent to the event bus, and the components subscribed to it receive it.

The product catalog component is interested in the **ItemRemovedFromCart** event. The component updates the product's availability and stock information when receiving the event. If the product was previously out of stock, the product catalog component emits a **ProductBackInStock** event, which the shopping cart component receives. The shopping cart component updates the user interface to show the product as available again.

Scenario 3: User places an order

The shopping cart component emits an **OrderPlaced** event when a user places an order. The event contains order details, such as user, product, and payment information. The event is sent to the event bus, and the components subscribed to it receive it.

The order processing component is interested in the **OrderPlaced** event. When the event is received, the order processing component validates the order details and initiates payment processing. If the payment is successful, the order processing component emits an **OrderCompleted** event, which the shopping cart component receives. The shopping cart component clears the user's cart and updates the user interface to show the order status as completed.

In summary, event-based communication promotes loose coupling among components, and each component operates independently.

Events drive the system's behavior, and components react to specific events per their functionality. The event-based communication model enables the system to handle changes easily, scale efficiently, and maintain flexibility.

Event ordering and idempotence

Event ordering and idempotence are essential concepts in event-driven architecture that ensure the correct processing of events and prevent unintended consequences of duplicate operations. Event ordering refers to the order in which the system processes events. In some cases, the order in which events are received and processed can affect the outcome of the system. Therefore, it is essential to ensure that events are processed in the correct order. Event ordering is especially important in scenarios where multiple events modify the system's state, and the order in which they occur can impact the result.

For example, consider a banking system where two events occur: a deposit of $100 and a withdrawal of $50. If the withdrawal is processed before the deposit, the account balance will be incorrect, and the withdrawal may fail due to insufficient funds. To avoid such issues, events must be processed in the correct order to ensure that the account balance is updated correctly.

To manage event ordering, systems use time-stamping events or a sequence number to order events. When events are time-stamped, the system ensures that events are processed in the order they were received.

Idempotence refers to the property of an operation where multiple identical operations have the same effect as a single operation. In other words, if an operation is idempotent, performing it multiple times will only change the system's state after the first time it was performed.

For example, consider a system that processes orders for a pizza restaurant. If a customer orders twice, the system should only process once to avoid duplicate orders. If the order processing operation is idempotent, the system can ensure that the order is processed only once, even if the customer accidentally places the order twice.

Idempotence is achieved by designing repeatable operations without changing the system's state. To make an operation idempotent, the system must ensure that the operation has no side effects when performed multiple times with the same input. In other words, the system should perform the operation once, store the result, and then return the same result when the same operation is performed again.

In summary, event ordering and idempotence are important concepts in event-driven architecture that ensure the correct processing of events and prevent unintended consequences of duplicate operations. Event-driven systems can ensure consistency, reliability, and fault tolerance by managing event ordering and designing idempotent operations.

Event schema

In event-driven architecture, events communicate between different components or services. An event schema is a way of defining the structure and content of an event, which is crucial for ensuring that all components can interpret the event correctly.

An event schema typically includes the following information:

- **Event type**: This is a string that identifies the type of event. It should be unique and descriptive so that other components can easily understand what the event represents.
- **Payload**: This is the data that accompanies the event. It can be in any format, such as JSON or XML, and contains relevant information that must be conveyed to other components. For example, in an e-commerce system, an order placed event might have a payload that includes the customer's name, email address, and ordered items.
- **Metadata**: This includes any additional information about the event, such as the timestamp, the source of the event, and any other contextual information that might be relevant.

Defining an event schema is important for several reasons:

- **It enables interoperability**: When different components in a system communicate using events, they all must understand the events in the same way. An event schema provides a standardized way of defining events, ensuring all components can interpret them correctly.
- **It simplifies event handling**: By defining the structure and content of events, it is easier to handle them in code. For example, if the payload of an event is always in a specific format, components that handle that event can assume that

the payload will always be structured in a certain way, which makes it easier to parse and use.

- **It makes testing easier**: By defining the expected structure of events, it is easier to write tests that verify that events are being produced and consumed correctly.

The following is a simple example of an event schema:

```
{
  "type": "order_placed",
    "payload": {
 "customer_name": "John Smith",
        "customer_email": "john@example.com",
        "items": [
            {
                "name": "Widget",
                "quantity": 2,
                "price": 10.00
            },
            {
                "name": "Gadget",
                "quantity": 1,
                "price": 20.00
            }
        ]
    },
  "metadata": {
        "timestamp": "2023-03-14T10:00:00Z",
        "source": "checkout-service"
    }
}
```

In the preceding example, the event type is **`order_placed`**, and the payload includes information about the customer and the items they ordered. The metadata includes the timestamp and the source of the event. Components handling this event can use this schema to ensure they interpret it correctly.

Event sourcing

Event sourcing is a popular data storage pattern used in event-driven architectures, where a sequence of events determines the state of a system. Instead of persisting in the system's current state, event sourcing involves storing all changes to the system as a series of immutable events.

The following algorithm outlines the steps involved in event sourcing:

- **Capture an event**: Whenever a change occurs in the system, create an event that captures the change's details. Each event should have a unique identifier and a timestamp and be immutable.
- **Store the event**: Store the event in an event store, a database for storing events. Each event should be appended to the end of the event stream.
- **Replay events**: To reconstruct the system state at any point, replay all events in the order they were stored. To do this, read events from the event store starting from the earliest event, and apply each event to a state object, which starts as an empty object.
- **Generate current state**: After replaying all events, the resulting state object represents the system's current state.

Let us consider an example of a banking system to illustrate the event sourcing pattern. Suppose a user deposits $100 into their account, followed by a withdrawal of $50. In an event-sourced system, each transaction would be captured as an event, like **`DepositEvent`** and **`WithdrawalEvent`**. Each event would contain relevant data, such as the amount deposited or withdrawn, the account number, and a timestamp.

These events would be stored in an event store, each appended to the end of the stream. When the system needs to determine the current account balance, it would replay all events in the order they were stored and then apply each event to an empty state object. The state object would track the current account balance, which can be easily retrieved once all events have been replayed.

One of the main benefits of event sourcing is that it provides a complete audit trail of all changes made to the system. Because events are immutable, they cannot be changed or deleted, ensuring data integrity. Additionally, the pattern supports temporal queries, enabling querying the state of the system at a specific point in time by replaying only events up to that point.

However, event sourcing has some tradeoffs, because all changes are stored as events, the amount of data to be stored can be significant, leading to storage costs. Also, replaying events can be slow and resource-intensive, particularly for large systems with many events.

The following is an example of how to implement event sourcing:

1. First, let us define a simple event class that represents a bank account transaction:

```
public class BankAccountTransactionEvent
{
    public Guid Id { get; set; }
    public string AccountNumber { get; set; }
    public decimal Amount { get; set; }
    public DateTime Timestamp { get; set; }
}
```

2. Next, we will define an event store interface that our implementation will adhere to:

```
public interface IEventStore
{
    void AppendEvent(BankAccountTransactionEvent @
    event);
    IEnumerable<BankAccountTransactionEvent>
    GetEventsForAccount(string accountNumber);
}
```

3. Now, let us implement the event store using a simple in-memory list to store events:

```
public class InMemoryEventStore : IEventStore
{
    private readonly
    List<BankAccountTransactionEvent> _events = new
    List<BankAccountTransactionEvent>();
```

```
        public void AppendEvent(BankAccountTransaction-
        Event @event)
        {
            _events.Add(@event);
        }

        public IEnumerable<BankAccountTransactionEvent>
        GetEventsForAccount(string accountNumber)
        {
            return _events.Where(e => e.AccountNumber ==
            accountNumber);
        }
    }
```

4. Finally, let us create a bank account class that uses the event store to implement its behavior:

```
public class BankAccount
{
    private readonly IEventStore _eventStore;
    private decimal _balance;

    public BankAccount(string accountNumber,
    IEventStore eventStore)
    {
        AccountNumber = accountNumber;
        _eventStore = eventStore;
    }

    public string AccountNumber { get; }

    public decimal GetBalance()
    {
        return _balance;
    }

    public void Deposit(decimal amount)
```

```
        {
            var @event = new BankAccountTransactionEvent
            {
                Id = Guid.NewGuid(),
                AccountNumber = AccountNumber,
                Amount = amount,
                Timestamp = DateTime.UtcNow
            };
            _eventStore.AppendEvent(@event);
            _balance += amount;
        }

        public void Withdraw(decimal amount)
        {
            if (_balance < amount)
            {
                throw new InvalidOperationException("In-
                sufficient funds.");
            }
            var @event = new BankAccountTransactionEvent
            {
                Id = Guid.NewGuid(),
                AccountNumber = AccountNumber,
                Amount = -amount,
                Timestamp = DateTime.UtcNow
            };
            _eventStore.AppendEvent(@event);
            _balance -= amount;
        }

        public void RebuildFromEvents()
        {
            foreach (var @event in _eventStore.
            GetEventsForAccount(AccountNumber))
```

```
                {
                    _balance += @event.Amount;
                }
            }
        }
```

5. In this implementation, the **BankAccount** class maintains a private field for the current balance and mutates it based on deposit and withdrawal events that persist in the event store. If needed, the **RebuildFromEvents** method allows the account to be reconstructed from past events.

In conclusion, event sourcing is a powerful pattern that provides benefits such as audibility, data integrity, and temporal querying. Due to its tradeoffs, it may be a better fit for some use cases, but it is a valuable option to consider when designing event-driven systems.

Command Query Responsibility Segregation

Command Query Responsibility Segregation (CQRS) is an architectural pattern commonly used in event-driven architectures to address the challenges of handling write and read operations on data. In a traditional architecture, a single model is responsible for handling both write and read operations, which can lead to issues such as scalability, performance, and complexity.

CQRS addresses these issues by separating the responsibilities of handling write and read operations into two distinct models or services. The write model, or the command side, handles operations that change the system's state, such as creating, updating, or deleting data. The read model, or the query side, handles operations that retrieve data from the system.

Let us consider an example of a blogging platform. The same model would create and retrieve blog posts in a traditional architecture. However, this can lead to slow performance when retrieving many blog posts or difficulty scaling the system to handle high write and read loads.

With CQRS, the write model would handle creating, updating, and deleting blog posts. Each of these operations would result in an event being emitted that describes the change that occurred, and these events would be persisted in an event store.

The read model would then handle operations that retrieve data, such as querying for a list of blog posts. The read model would subscribe to the events emitted by the write model and update its data store to reflect the changes. This allows the read model to provide fast and efficient data querying without dealing with the complexity of handling writes.

One of the main benefits of CQRS is that it allows for more flexible and scalable architectures. The write and read models can be scaled independently to handle high loads of either writes or reads. Additionally, the separation of concerns makes the system easier to reason with and can simplify testing and maintenance.

However, CQRS also comes with some tradeoffs. The added complexity of separating the write and read models can make the system more difficult to design and implement. Additionally, because the read model needs to be updated based on events emitted by the write model, there can be some latency between when a change is made and when it is reflected in the read model.

Overall, CQRS is a powerful pattern that can provide benefits such as scalability, flexibility, and simplified reasoning about the system. However, it may not be the best fit for every use case due to its tradeoffs.

Conclusion

In this chapter, we have learned event-driven architecture emphasizes the use of events as the fundamental components of the system, allowing different parts to communicate via an event bus or message queue. Event producers generate events that capture changes or updates in the system and publish them to a specific topic. The topics categorize events that consumers can subscribe to, enabling them to receive notifications of changes in the system. Event consumers subscribe to one or more topics and receive events published on those topics.

We also learned that the event bus facilitates communication between producers and consumers, allowing them to exchange messages asynchronously. Loose coupling is a fundamental principle of event-driven architecture. Changes can be made without affecting other components, and different parts of the system do not depend on each other.

Event-based communication is more flexible and scalable than traditional request-response communication, making it ideal for highly distributed systems. Event ordering and idempotence are crucial factors in event-driven architecture to ensure that events are processed correctly, and identical events do not lead to unintended consequences.

The event schema defines events' format, properties, and data types, promoting interoperability between different system components. Event sourcing and **Command Query Responsibility Segregation** (**CQRS**) are additional patterns used in event-driven architecture to improve data consistency and system scalability.

In the next chapter, you will discover how to create a strong event-driven system through design and implementation. You will learn how to identify which events to produce and consume, how to create a schema, an event bus, and other critical components to create an event-driven system.

Join our book's Discord space

Join the book's Discord Workspace for Latest updates, Offers, Tech happenings around the world, New Release and Sessions with the Authors:

https://discord.bpbonline.com

CHAPTER 3
Designing Event-Driven Systems

Introduction

Designing event-driven systems is the process of creating a solution where events are at the center, and communication happens through them. This approach allows for quick reaction to events, the ability to handle many events at the same time, and independent components. The main objective of designing event-driven systems is to build a system that can process and respond to events in real time.

Structure

In this chapter, we will cover the following topics:

- Identifying the events
- Defining the event schema
- Choosing an event bus
- Deciding on event consumers
- Addressing event ordering and idempotence
- Testing and monitoring
- Fault tolerance

Objectives

This process aims to design and implement a robust event-driven architecture system. This involves identifying the types of events to be produced and consumed, creating an event schema, choosing an event bus, and designing event consumers that are scalable and loosely coupled. The process also includes implementing event-based communication, addressing event ordering and idempotence, testing and monitoring the system, and implementing fault tolerance mechanisms to handle failures and errors.

Identifying the events

To design an effective **event-driven architecture** (**EDA**) system, it is crucial to determine the types of events produced and consumed by the system. This involves identifying the different types of events that are likely to occur in the system and how they will be generated, consumed, and processed. The following are the detailed steps to determine the types of events:

Identify the business processes

The first step is to identify the key business processes in the system. Identifying business processes is an essential step in developing an EDA system, and this step helps determine the different events that may occur within the system. Business processes are the workflows that define how an organization operates and creates value for its customers. These workflows involve a series of tasks that different actors, such as employees or machines, execute.

For example, let us consider an e-commerce website that sells products online. The business processes involved in this website may include:

- **Product ordering**: A customer orders a product through the website.
- **Payment processing**: The website processes the payment for the order.
- **Order fulfilment**: The website fulfils the order by shipping the product to the customer.
- **Inventory management**: The website manages the inventory of products to ensure that products are available for ordering.

- **Customer service**: The website provides customer service, such as handling returns and answering customer inquiries.

Each business process generates events that could be captured and processed within an EDA system. For example, an event could be generated when a customer orders or the payment is processed. By identifying the business processes, we can determine the events relevant to the system and design the EDA system to capture and process these events. This helps ensure that the system is designed to meet the organization's specific needs and can provide value by improving the efficiency and effectiveness of the business processes.

Identify the actions and events

After identifying the business processes, the next step is to identify the actions and events that occur within each process. An action is any activity or operation that occurs as part of the business process, while an event is any occurrence that triggers or results from an action. Here is an example to illustrate the process:

Let us consider a simple example of an e-commerce website. One of the business processes on this website is the checkout process. The checkout process involves several actions such as adding items to the cart, entering billing, and shipping information, and completing the payment.

Now, we need to identify the events that occur during this process. The events include the following:

- **Item added to cart**: This event occurs when users add an item to their shopping cart.
- **Payment submitted**: This event occurs when users submit their payment information to complete the checkout process.
- **Order confirmation**: This event occurs when the user receives confirmation that their order has been placed successfully.
- **Order shipped**: This event occurs when the order has been shipped to the customer.

By identifying these events, we can design an event-driven system that responds to each event and triggers the appropriate action. For example, when the *"Payment submitted"* event occurs, the system can trigger the payment processing action to complete the transaction. Similarly, when the *"Order shipped"* event occurs, the system can notify the user with the shipping details.

Identifying the actions and events is crucial in designing an event-driven system that can handle complex business processes and respond to events in real-time. By understanding the events within each business process, we can build a flexible, scalable system that can respond to changing business needs.

Identifying triggers

It is an important aspect of understanding how a process or system works. By identifying the triggers, you can gain insight into why certain actions occur and how to modify or optimize the system.

For example, let us say you are developing an e-commerce website. You want to track when users purchase so you can analyze their behavior and improve the user experience. In this case, the trigger would be when a user completes a purchase on your website.

Another example could be a home security system. The trigger for this system could be when a motion sensor is triggered, indicating that someone has entered the house.

In both cases, the trigger is an event that initiates a specific activity or action. By identifying the trigger, you can take steps to optimize or improve the process. For example, if you notice that users are not completing purchases on your website, you can analyze the trigger and change the user experience to encourage more purchases.

Identifying events attributes

Determining the types of events, the system will produce and consume is essential in designing an event-driven architecture. Events are occurrences or changes in the system that need to be processed and acted upon by different components. Identifying the right types of events is crucial to ensure that the system can function efficiently and meet the business requirements.

To determine the types of events the system will produce and consume, you need to start by understanding the business domain and the specific problem you are trying to solve. You can do this by conducting a domain analysis, which involves identifying the key entities, processes, and business rules that govern the system. This analysis will help you identify the different types of events that are relevant to the system.

For example, let us say you are designing an e-commerce website that allows customers to purchase products online. The key entities in this system are customers, products, orders, and payments. The processes involved in this system include browsing products, adding items to the cart, entering payment information, and confirming the order. The business rules include pricing, discounts, shipping, and taxes.

Based on this analysis, you can identify the following types of events:

- `ProductAddedToCart`: This event is produced when a customer adds a product to their shopping cart. The event includes information about the product, the customer, and the cart.
- `PaymentReceived`: This event is produced when a payment is received for an order. The event includes information about the order, the customer, and the payment.
- `OrderConfirmed`: This event is produced when an order is confirmed by the customer. The event includes information about the order and the customer.
- `ProductSoldOut`: This event is produced when a product is sold out and unavailable for purchase. The event includes information about the product and the inventory.
- `OrderCancelled`: This event is produced when an order is cancelled by the customer. The event includes information about the order and the customer.

Once you have identified the types of events, you need to determine how the system will produce and consume them. This involves identifying the components that will produce the events and the components that will consume them. You also need to decide on the format of the events and how they will be transmitted between the components.

In summary, determining the types of events the system will produce and consume requires a thorough understanding of the business domain and the problem you are trying to solve. By identifying the key entities, processes, and business rules, you can identify the relevant types of events and design a system that can efficiently handle them.

Categorizing events

Categorizing events is an essential step in designing an EDA system. Categorizing events means grouping events based on their type, source, and purpose, which helps understand the system's behavior and design its components accordingly. In the context of an e-commerce website, categorizing events can help identify the various types of user interactions, such as product views, cart updates, and purchases, and analyzing the user behavior to improve the website's functionality and user experience.

Let us consider an example of an e-commerce website that sells electronics. The website has various components, such as a homepage, product page, cart, and checkout page. The website aims to enable customers to browse and purchase products seamlessly. Here are some examples of events that could occur in the e-commerce website:

- **User visits the homepage**: This event occurs when a user accesses the website's homepage. This event can be categorized as a page view event.
- **User searches for a product**: This event occurs when a user searches for a specific product on the website. This event can be categorized as a search event.
- **User views a product**: This event occurs when a user clicks on a product and views its details. This event can be categorized as a product view event.
- **User adds a product to the cart**: This event occurs when a user adds a product to their cart. This event can be categorized as a cart update event.
- **User removes a product from the cart**: This event occurs when a user removes a product from their cart. This event can also be categorized as a cart update event.
- **User proceeds to checkout**: This event occurs when a user clicks on the checkout button. This event can be categorized as a checkout event.
- **User completes a purchase**: This event occurs when a user completes the checkout process and places an order. This event can be categorized as a purchase event.

By categorizing these events, we can understand the users' behavior and interactions with the website. For example, we can track the most popular products, the number of products added to the cart, and the number of purchases. This information can be used to improve the website's functionality and user experience.

Furthermore, categorizing events can also help identify potential issues and bugs on the website. For example, if a significant number of users add a product to their cart but do not complete the checkout process, it could indicate issues with the checkout page's design or functionality. By analyzing the events, we can identify the root cause of the issue and take steps to address it.

In conclusion, categorizing events is crucial in designing an EDA system for an e-commerce website. By categorizing the events, we can understand the users' behavior and interactions with the website, identify potential issues, and improve the website's functionality and user experience.

Defining the event schema

Event schemas enable different components to communicate effectively by ensuring that events are consistently formatted and contain the expected data. This consistency makes it easier to integrate new components into the system and modify existing ones without causing disruptions.

To define an event schema, follow these steps:

- **Define the event name**: Give the event a descriptive name that identifies the type of event that is occurring. For example, "UserCreated" or "OrderFulfilled".
- **Define the event properties**: List the properties of the event and their types. Each property should describe a specific piece of data related to the event. For example, if the event is "UserCreated", the properties might include "userId" (a string), "email" (a string), "name" (a string), and "createdAt" (a timestamp).
- **Define optional properties**: If there are any optional properties that might be included in the event, indicate this in the schema. For example, if the "UserCreated" event might also include a "phoneNumber" property, this should be listed as an optional property.
- **Define metadata**: Include any relevant metadata to the event, such as the timestamp of when the event occurred or the source of the event.
- **Define the schema format**: Choose a format for the schema, such as JSON Schema or Avro Schema.
- **Store the schema**: Store the schema in a schema registry or other central location that can be accessed by other components in the event-driven architecture.

When defining the event schema, it is important to consider the needs of the system and the components that will be processing the event. The schema should be designed to ensure that the event data is consistent and can be easily processed by all components that need to consume it.

Let us define an event schema using an example of a `UserCreated` event:

Event name: "UserCreated"

Event properties:

- `userId`: a string that uniquely identifies the user.
- `email`: a string that contains the user's email address.
- `firstName`: a string that contains the user's first name.
- `lastName`: a string that contains the user's last name.
- `createdAt`: a timestamp that indicates when the user was created.

These properties would be defined with a specific data type, such as a string or a timestamp.

Optional properties:

- `phoneNumber`: a string that contains the user's phone number (optional).

Metadata:

- `eventId`: a unique identifier for the event
- `eventType`: the type of event, which in this case is "UserCreated".
- `eventTimestamp`: a timestamp that indicates when the event occurred.

Schema Format: JSON Schema

Here is an example JSON schema for the "UserCreated" event:

```
{
  "type": "object",
  "required": ["userId", "email", "firstName", "lastName",
  "createdAt"],
  "properties": {
    "userId": {
```

```
      "type": "string"
    },
    "email": {
      "type": "string",
      "format": "email"
    },
    "firstName": {
      "type": "string"
    },
    "lastName": {
      "type": "string"
    },
    "createdAt": {
      "type": "string",
      "format": "date-time"
    },
    "phoneNumber": {
      "type": "string"
    }
  },
  "additionalProperties": false,
  "definitions": {
    "eventId": {
      "type": "string"
    },
    "eventType": {
      "type": "string",
      "const": "UserCreated"
    },
    "eventTimestamp": {
      "type": "string",
      "format": "date-time"
    }
```

```
    }

}
```

This schema defines the structure and content of the UserCreated event, including the required and optional properties, metadata, and schema format. This schema can be stored in a schema registry and used by other components in the event-driven architecture to ensure that the UserCreated event is processed consistently across the system.

Choosing an event bus

Choosing the right event bus is critical for the success of an event-driven architecture. The event bus is the system's core, facilitating communication and data transfer between various components. An appropriate event bus can guarantee the system's dependability, scalability, and efficiency. Conversely, a wrong choice of event bus may result in problems such as message loss, delays, and system crashes. Thus, carefully examining and assessing different event bus alternatives is necessary to create a robust event-driven architecture.

Let us consider an example of an e-commerce website that needs to handle many online transactions, product updates, and customer interactions. Here are some factors to consider when selecting an event bus for this use case:

- **Scalability**: The event bus should be able to handle a high volume of messages and scale horizontally as the website grows. In our use case, we may expect a large number of product updates, customer interactions, and transactions to be processed in real-time, so scalability is a critical factor.
- **Reliability**: The event bus should be reliable and ensure that events are delivered without loss or duplication, even in the face of network failures or other disruptions. Reliability is especially important in an e-commerce website where lost or duplicated events could cause significant customer and business problems.
- **Compatibility**: An event bus acts as a communication channel between different services or components, enabling them to communicate without tight coupling. Supporting standard messaging formats and protocols enhances compatibility, making it easier for diverse systems to interact seamlessly.

- **Ease of use**: The event bus should be easy to use and manage, with good documentation and support. Ease of use is critical for developers to build and maintain the event-driven architecture efficiently.
- **Performance**: The event bus should be fast and responsive, with low latency and high throughput. Performance is essential to ensure real-time updates and transactions are processed quickly and efficiently.
- **Security**: The event bus should provide adequate security measures such as encryption, authentication, and authorization to protect sensitive information.
- **Cost**: The cost of the event bus should be reasonable and aligned with the needs and budget of the e-commerce website. High costs could limit the ability of the website to scale and grow.

Using RabbitMQ as an event bus, an e-commerce website can benefit from its high scalability, reliability, and performance. RabbitMQ's ability to handle a large number of concurrent connections and its support for various messaging protocols make it an ideal choice for an event-driven architecture. Additionally, RabbitMQ's ease of use and excellent documentation make it a popular choice among developers.

Deciding on event consumers

In an event-driven architecture, consumers are pivotal as they are responsible for processing and handling events generated by various system components. These consumers facilitate loose coupling between the different components, which enables greater flexibility, scalability, and reliability in the system. A well-designed and properly implemented consumer can enhance the system's efficiency and responsiveness, while a poorly implemented one can result in delays, errors, and loss of messages. As a result, it is crucial to carefully consider and evaluate consumer design and implementation to ensure the success of an event-driven architecture.

Creating a well-designed consumer in an event-driven architecture involves several key steps:

1. **Identify the use case and requirements**: In an ecommerce website, the consumer might need to handle events such as **`OrderPlaced`**, **`PaymentReceived`**, or **`ItemShipped`**.

Understanding the requirements for processing these events, such as validating the data, updating the order status, and sending notifications to the customer is essential.

2. **Choose the right technology stack**: For an ecommerce website, a technology stack that can handle high volumes of events, such as Rabbit MQ, might be appropriate. The chosen technology stack should be scalable and fault tolerant.
3. **Implement fault-tolerant and scalable design**: The consumer should be designed to handle failures and ensure that events are processed reliably. This could involve implementing features such as distributed processing, message acknowledgments, and retries.
4. **Properly handle errors and exceptions**: The consumer should handle errors and exceptions appropriately, with proper logging and notification mechanisms in place to ensure that issues are identified and addressed promptly.
5. **Test and optimize performance**: Proper testing and performance optimization are essential for ensuring the consumer functions correctly under load and can handle high volumes of events. This involves load testing, tuning configurations, and measuring and monitoring system metrics.

By following these steps, developers can create a well-designed consumer that meets the requirements of an ecommerce website and performs optimally within an event-driven architecture.

Addressing event ordering and idempotence

EDA rely heavily on the flow of events to communicate changes and state updates between different services or systems. As a result, ensuring the correct order of events and maintaining idempotence is crucial for implementing an EDA.

Let us have a detailed discussion about event ordering and idempotence:

- **Event ordering**: One of the key challenges in event-driven systems is ensuring that the sequence of events is maintained. The order of events can impact the system's state, and if the events are processed out of order, it can lead to data inconsistencies and unpredictable behavior. For example, consider a scenario where a user updates their profile and then places an order. If the order event is processed before the profile update event, the order may be placed with incorrect user information, resulting in incorrect billing and shipping details. Addressing event ordering ensures that events are processed in the correct order, and the system state is maintained consistently.

- **Idempotence**: Idempotence is the property of an operation in which applying the same operation multiple times does not change the system state beyond the initial application. In an event-driven system, idempotence ensures that the system remains consistent, even if the same event is processed multiple times. Without idempotence, duplicate events can cause the system to execute the same operation multiple times, leading to unexpected results, such as overcharging a customer or deleting the wrong record. Addressing idempotence ensures that events are processed only once, and the system remains consistent.

Addressing event ordering and idempotence in an EDA ensures that the events are processed correctly, the system state is maintained consistently, and the system operates reliably despite errors and failures. Addressing these aspects also helps to reduce the chances of data inconsistencies and other issues that can impact the reliability and accuracy of the system.

Let us take an example of an e-commerce website to understand the importance of addressing event ordering and idempotence in event-driven architecture.

Suppose a user place an order for a product on the website. This generates an "order created" event published to a message broker, such as Rabbit MQ, which sends the event to multiple services in the system. These services may include order processing, inventory management, shipping, and payment processing.

Now, let us assume that the **order created** event is not processed in the correct order due to a network delay or other issues. As a result, the inventory management service receives the event before the payment processing service. The inventory management service checks the availability of the product and finds that there is sufficient stock. However, before the payment processing service can verify the payment details, the inventory management service reserves the product, reducing the stock level. Later, when the payment processing service receives the event, it may discover that the payment was declined or failed, and it cannot authorize the payment. At this point, the inventory management service has already reserved the product. The payment has not been authorized, leading to an inconsistent system state where the stock level is reduced, but the payment has not been processed.

To avoid such a scenario, addressing event ordering ensures that the services process the events in the correct order, maintaining a consistent system state.

Now, let us consider the importance of addressing idempotence in the same scenario. Suppose the "order created" event is processed multiple times due to network issues or other failures. As a result, the inventory management service may reserve the product multiple times, leading to an incorrect stock level and overbooking of the product. Similarly, the payment processing service may process the payment multiple times, leading to overcharging the customer and causing other issues.

Addressing idempotence ensures that the system remains consistent, even if the same event is processed multiple times. By assigning a unique identifier to each event and checking it against a database to ensure that the event has not been processed before, the system can avoid duplicate events and maintain consistency.

In summary, addressing event ordering and idempotence in event-driven architecture is crucial for maintaining a consistent and reliable system. Failure to address these aspects can lead to data inconsistencies, incorrect system behavior, and other issues that can impact the reliability and accuracy of the system.

Testing and monitoring

Testing and monitoring are crucial components of any event-driven system. Event-driven systems are designed to react to events in real-time, requiring rigorous testing and monitoring to ensure that they function properly and deliver accurate results.

The following are some of the reasons why testing and monitoring are important in event-driven systems:

- **Ensures correct functionality**: Testing is necessary to ensure the system functions correctly and delivers accurate results. It can help identify any issues or bugs in the system before it is deployed, minimizing the risk of downtime or other issues.

- **Enables quick response to issues**: Monitoring allows developers to quickly identify any issues or bugs in the system, enabling them to respond quickly and minimize downtime or other issues.
- **Improves scalability**: Testing and monitoring are essential to ensure that the system is scalable and can handle increasing volumes of data and events. This allows the system to grow and adapt to changing demands over time.
- **Enhances user experience**: Testing and monitoring can help identify any issues or bugs that could impact the user experience. This allows developers to fix these issues before they affect the user, improving the overall user experience.
- **Enables continuous improvement**: Testing and monitoring provide valuable feedback to developers, enabling them to continuously improve the system and make it more efficient and effective over time.

Further let us understand the importance of testing and monitoring in event-driven systems using below given example of stock market data.

Imagine you are developing a real-time system that processes stock market data. This system is designed to receive events such as new stock prices, trade orders, and other market-related data, and then make real-time decisions based on this data. The system must be fast, scalable, and reliable to ensure traders can make informed decisions based on the latest market data.

Testing is critical to ensure that this system works correctly and is error-free. For example, you need to test the system's ability to handle different events, such as new stock prices, trade orders, and other market-related data. You also need to test the system's ability to make real-time decisions based on this data, ensuring that the system can handle high volumes of data without crashing or slowing down.

To test the system, you can create a series of test cases that simulate different scenarios, such as a sudden increase in trading volume or unexpected changes in stock prices. You can then run these test cases to see how the system responds and identify any errors or bugs. By identifying these issues during testing, you can fix them before the system goes live, minimizing the risk of downtime or other issues.

Monitoring is equally important in an event-driven system. Once the system is live, you must monitor it to ensure it performs correctly and delivers accurate results. For example, you need to monitor the system's response time to ensure it processes events in real-time. You also need to monitor the system's error rate to identify any issues that could impact the system's reliability.

You can use tools like ELK Stack for log analysis, Prometheus and Grafana for metrics platforms, and real-time dashboards in your event-driven system. ELK Stack helps you process and visualize log data, Prometheus collects and queries metrics, and Grafana provides interactive visualizations, allowing you to monitor the system's performance, diagnose issues, and gain insights into its behavior. These tools allow you to track the system's performance in real-time, making it easier to identify issues and respond quickly. For example, if the system's response time suddenly increases, you can investigate the issue and take steps to fix it before it affects the system's reliability.

In summary, testing and monitoring are critical components of event-driven systems. They help ensure the system functions correctly, responds quickly to issues, and delivers accurate results. By testing the system before it goes live and monitoring it once it is live, you can ensure that traders can access the latest market data, helping them make informed decisions and stay ahead of the competition.

Fault tolerance

Fault tolerance is critical to EDA because it enables systems to continue operating despite faults or failures. This topic will explain the importance of fault tolerance in event-driven architecture and how it helps ensure systems' reliability, availability, and scalability.

Event-driven architecture is a design pattern that emphasizes the use of events to trigger and coordinate the flow of information within a system. In an event-driven architecture, events can be generated by a variety of sources, including user interactions, sensors, and external systems. These events are processed by one or more event handlers, which can trigger additional events or perform other actions based on the information contained in the event.

In this discussion, we will delve into the key feature of fault tolerance, highlighting its significance in ensuring system reliability and uninterrupted operation even in the presence of failures or errors:

- **Ensures continuity of operations**: Fault tolerance is essential for ensuring the continuity of operations in event-driven architecture. In EDA, events trigger actions and coordinate the information flow between system components. If an event handler fails, it can disrupt the flow of events and cause the system to stop functioning correctly.

By implementing fault-tolerant mechanisms in EDA systems, such as redundant event handlers, the system can continue to operate even if one or more event handlers fail. This ensures that the system remains operational and available for use, even in the face of faults or failures.

For example, a fault-tolerant EDA system might include multiple instances of an event handler, with each instance running on a separate server. If one instance fails, the system can automatically switch to another instance, ensuring that the system continues to function without interruption.

- **Increases reliability**: Fault tolerance also increases the reliability of event-driven architecture systems. EDA systems rely heavily on the correct processing of events to trigger actions and coordinate the flow of information. If an event is lost or incorrectly processed due to a failure or fault, it can result in significant errors or disruptions to the system.

  By implementing fault-tolerant mechanisms in EDA systems, such as event replay mechanisms, the system can ensure that events are correctly processed even in the face of failures or faults. For example, an EDA system might include an event replay mechanism that can detect and replay events that were not correctly processed due to a failure or fault, ensuring that the system operates correctly.

- **Improves availability**: Fault tolerance also improves the availability of event-driven architecture systems. Availability refers to the amount of time that a system is operational and available for use. In many industries, high availability is critical to business operations. Fault-tolerant EDA systems are designed to ensure the system remains available despite failures or faults.

  For example, a fault-tolerant EDA system might include automatic failover mechanisms to detect failure and switch to a backup system without interruption. This ensures that the system remains available and operational even during a failure.

- **Enhances scalability**: Fault tolerance is also essential for ensuring the scalability of event-driven architecture systems.

Scalability refers to the ability of a system to handle increasing volumes of data and events. EDA systems can generate many events, and as the volume of events increases, the system must be able to handle the additional load.

By implementing fault-tolerant mechanisms in EDA systems, such as load balancing and automatic scaling, the system can handle increasing volumes of data and events without overloading or failing. For example, an EDA system might include load balancing mechanisms that distribute events across multiple event handlers, ensuring the system can handle many events without overloading.

- **Ensures data integrity**: Finally, fault tolerance ensures data integrity in event-driven architecture systems. Data integrity refers to the accuracy and consistency of data within a system. In EDA systems, events can contain critical data that must be processed.

Conclusion

In conclusion, the design of event-driven systems necessitates a distinctive approach that places events at the core of communication. This approach empowers the system to respond rapidly to events, manage multiple events simultaneously, and have independent components. The primary objective of this process is to build a system capable of processing and reacting to events in real-time.

To accomplish this objective, it is imperative to recognize the types of events that will be produced and consumed, establish an event schema, choose an event bus, create event consumers that are scalable and loosely coupled, and implement event-based communication. Additionally, it is essential to tackle event ordering and idempotence, test and monitor the system, and integrate fault tolerance mechanisms to handle failures and errors.

In the next chapter, we will walk you through the implementation of event-driven architecture using RabbitMQ messaging system and the .NET platform. It will provide a detailed insight into the functionalities and capabilities of RabbitMQ and .NET for developing event-driven systems. Following this implementation, you can create an event-driven system project in .NET with the help of RabbitMQ libraries.

Chapter 4
RabbitMQ for Event-Driven Microservices

Introduction

Implementing event-driven ar chitecture with RabbitMQ and .NET will cover creating an event-driven system using the RabbitMQ messaging system and the .NET platform. It will give an in-depth understanding of the features and capabilities of RabbitMQ and .NET for building event-driven systems. This implementation will teach you how to set up an Event-Driven System Project in .NET using RabbitMQ libraries.

Structure

In this chapter, we will cover the following topics:

- Advantages of RabbitMQ and .NET
- RabbitMQ messaging patterns and concepts
- RabbitMQ implementation for building event-driven .NET applications

Objectives

This chapter comprehensively explains RabbitMQ and .NET, highlighting their advantages in building event-driven systems. It covers various topics, starting with an introduction to message queues and RabbitMQ. The series then delves into RabbitMQ messaging patterns, including publish/subscribe and routing. It also provides an overview of .NET and its relevance in event-driven systems. Additionally, it offers guidance on setting up a .NET project specifically for event-driven architecture. Finally, the series provides instructions on utilizing .NET libraries for RabbitMQ to implement different messaging patterns and concepts.

Advantages of RabbitMQ and .NET

RabbitMQ is a widely used message broker with features like routing, publishing, subscribing, and request or response. By using RabbitMQ, developers can build highly scalable and reliable event-driven systems.

Another important component of event-driven systems is the development framework, which provides the programming languages, libraries, and tools needed to build and deploy applications. .NET is a popular development framework that supports multiple programming languages, including C#, F#, and Visual Basic. By using .NET, developers can take advantage of a large library and tool ecosystem, making building and deploying event-driven systems easier (refer to the following figure):

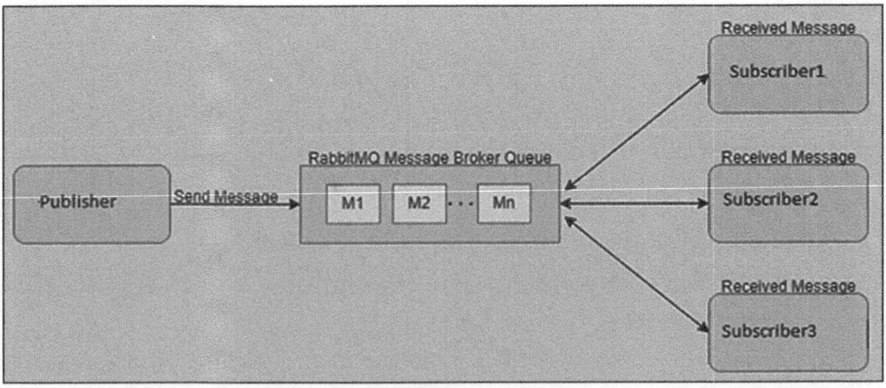

Figure 4.1: *RabbitMQ Message Broker*

There are several benefits of using RabbitMQ and .NET for building event-driven systems:

- **Scalability**: RabbitMQ is highly scalable and can handle large amounts of data and traffic. Using .NET, developers can build applications that can handle millions of events per second.
- **Flexibility**: RabbitMQ supports multiple messaging patterns and routing mechanisms, making it a flexible solution for building event-driven systems. .NET provides a wide range of programming languages and tools, giving developers the flexibility to choose the best language and tool for their application.
- **Reliability**: RabbitMQ provides reliable message delivery by guaranteeing that messages are delivered to their intended recipients. It also supports features like acknowledgments and message retries, which ensure that messages are not lost or discarded. .NET provides a robust runtime environment that can handle errors and exceptions, making applications more reliable.
- **Asynchronous programming**: RabbitMQ and .NET support asynchronous programming, which enables applications to process events in real-time without blocking the main thread. This improves application performance and responsiveness.
- **Ecosystem**: RabbitMQ and .NET have large ecosystems of libraries and tools that make it easier to build and deploy event-driven systems. For example, .NET provides libraries like MassTransit and NServiceBus, which abstract away many of the complexities of building event-driven systems.

  RabbitMQ is known for its simplicity, flexibility, and reliability compared to other message brokers. Apache Kafka, for example, is a popular message broker designed for handling high-volume, real-time data streams. While Kafka is highly performant, it can be complex to set up and manage. ActiveMQ is another popular message broker that supports many messaging patterns, but it can be less performant than RabbitMQ. Azure Service Bus is a managed message broker provided by Microsoft, but it can be more expensive than RabbitMQ.

RabbitMQ and .NET are popular choices for building event-driven systems, and many companies have successfully used them to build scalable and reliable systems. Here are some examples of companies that have used RabbitMQ and .NET for event-driven architectures:

- **SoundCloud**: SoundCloud is a popular music streaming service that uses RabbitMQ and .NET to handle its messaging infrastructure. The company uses RabbitMQ to process millions of events daily, including user interactions, content uploads, and music playback data. SoundCloud's event-driven architecture enables the company to scale its system and provide a seamless user experience to its customers.
- **Hopper**: Hopper is a travel booking app that uses RabbitMQ and .NET to manage its messaging infrastructure. The company uses RabbitMQ to process flight and hotel data from multiple sources and provide its users with real-time pricing and availability information. Hopper's event-driven architecture enables the company to process large amounts of data and provide fast and accurate results to its customers.
- **General Electric (GE)** is a multinational conglomerate that uses RabbitMQ and .NET to manage its messaging infrastructure across its many business units. GE uses RabbitMQ to handle machine-to-machine communication and process large amounts of data from sensors and other sources. GE's event-driven architecture enables the company to monitor and optimize its operations in real-time.
- **Stack overflow**: Stack Overflow is a popular Q&A website for programmers that uses RabbitMQ and .NET to manage its messaging infrastructure. The company uses RabbitMQ to process user interactions and provide real-time notifications to its users. Stack Overflow's event-driven architecture enables the company to scale its system and provide a seamless user experience to its millions of users.

These are just a few examples of companies successfully using RabbitMQ and .NET for event-driven systems. The combination of RabbitMQ's flexible messaging patterns, high performance, and reliability, along with .NET's robust framework and tooling, make them a powerful combination for building scalable and reliable systems.

RabbitMQ messaging patterns and concepts

RabbitMQ supports various messaging patterns that provide flexibility and versatility in designing messaging systems. These patterns help route messages between producers and consumers based on specific rules. Let us explore the most common messaging patterns supported by RabbitMQ:

- **Publish or subscribe:** The publish or subscribe pattern allows a message producer to send messages to an exchange, distributing them to multiple queues. Consumers interested in a particular topic or category can bind to the respective queues and receive messages. This pattern enables broadcasting messages to multiple consumers simultaneously.

  In RabbitMQ, the publish or subscribe pattern involves creating an exchange of type "fanout". When a producer publishes a message to the exchange, it gets distributed to all the queues bound to that exchange, and each consumer binds to a specific queue and receives a copy of the message.

  For example, in a microservices architecture, consider a scenario where a user registration service publishes an event whenever a new user is registered. Several other services, such as a notification service, analytics service, and email service, must be notified of this event. Using the publish or subscribe pattern, the user registration service publishes the event to an exchange, and the interested services subscribe to that exchange. Each service receives a copy of the event and can perform specific actions based on the event data.

- **Routing:** The routing pattern enables selective message routing based on message attributes. Producers send messages to an exchange, which routes them to specific queues based on routing rules defined by the exchange. These routing rules can be based on message headers, routing keys, or patterns.

  In RabbitMQ, the routing pattern involves creating an exchange of type "direct." Producers specify a routing key when sending a message, and the exchange routes the message to the queues with matching routing keys.

  For example, different queues can be created to process different trade orders in a stock trading system, such as "buy_ orders" and "sell_orders." Traders submitting buy orders will publish messages with a "buy" routing key, while those submitting sell orders will use the "sell." The routing logic in RabbitMQ routes the buy orders to the "buy_orders" queue and the sell orders to the "sell_orders" queue. This ensures the messages are delivered only to the appropriate queues for further processing by the respective components.

- **Request or response:** The request or response pattern facilitates synchronous communication between a client (requester) and a server (responder). A client sends a request message to a specific queue and waits for a response from the server. The server listens to the queue, processes the request, and responds to the client's designated callback queue.

  In RabbitMQ, the request or response pattern involves creating a temporary callback queue for each client request. The client includes a unique correlation ID in the request message, and the server includes the same correlation ID in the response message to associate them.

  For example, consider an e-commerce application where a customer places an order. The order management service can utilize the request or response pattern to send a request message to the payment service, asking it to process the payment. The payment service receives the request, processes the payment, and sends a response message to the order management service indicating whether the payment was successful. This synchronous communication allows the order management service to act appropriately based on the payment response.

- **Exchanges in RabbitMQ:** In RabbitMQ, exchanges are the key components that receive messages from producers and route them to queues based on specific rules. They act as intermediaries between producers and queues, determining the message's destination within the messaging system. Understanding the concepts of exchanges is crucial for designing efficient and flexible messaging patterns. Let us explore exchanges in more detail with an example:

  - **Exchange types:** RabbitMQ supports different exchanges to cater to message routing scenarios. The commonly used exchange types are:

    - **Direct exchange:** Messages are routed to queues using a matching routing key. For example, if a message is published with a routing key of "error," it will be delivered to queues bound to the exchange with the same routing key.

- **Fanout exchange:** Messages are broadcast to all queues bound to the exchange. Regardless of the routing key, all messages sent to a fanout exchange are delivered to all bound queues.
- **Topic exchange:** Messages are routed based on matching patterns defined by the routing key. Routing keys in a topic exchange are usually formed using words separated by dots. Queues can bind to the exchange using wildcard patterns to receive specific messages. For instance, a binding with a routing key pattern of "logs.*" will match messages with routing keys like "logs.info" or "logs.warning".
- **Header's exchange:** Messages are routed based on header attributes instead of routing keys. The exchange matches the headers in the message with bindings that specify desired header values.
- **Creating an exchange:** To create an exchange in RabbitMQ, specify the exchange's name and type. Exchanges can be created programmatically using RabbitMQ client libraries or through management tools like RabbitMQ Management UI. For example, let us consider a scenario with a messaging system consisting of a producer, exchanges, queues, and consumers. We will focus on a direct exchange named "my_direct_exchange".
- **Binding queues to the exchange:** To establish the routing path for messages, you need to bind queues to the exchange. Queues can be bound to the exchange with specific routing keys or patterns, depending on the exchange type.

  For example, in our scenario, we have two queues, "queue1" and "queue2", that need to be bound to the "my_direct_exchange". "queue1" is bound with a routing key "info", and "queue2" is bound with a routing key "error". This means that messages with the routing key "info" will be routed to "queue1", while messages with the routing key "error" will be routed to "queue2".

- **Publishing messages to the exchange:** The producer sends messages to the exchange rather than directly to the queues. When publishing a message, the producer specifies the exchange and the routing key.

  For example, the producer publishes a message with the routing key "info" to the "my_direct_exchange". RabbitMQ routes this message to "queue1" because it matches the routing key binding. Similarly, if the producer publishes a message with the routing key "error", it will be routed to "queue2". By utilizing exchanges, messages can be routed efficiently to the appropriate queues based on routing rules. This enables the decoupling of producers and consumers and the implementation of various messaging patterns such as publish or subscribe, routing, and request or response. Exchanges provide the flexibility and versatility required for building robust and scalable messaging systems with RabbitMQ.

- **Queues in RabbitMQ:** In RabbitMQ, queues are an integral part of the messaging system. They serve as buffers that hold messages until consumers consume them. Queues ensure reliable message delivery and decouple producers from consumers, allowing asynchronous communication between different system components. Let us delve into the concept of queues in more detail with an example:

  Imagine a scenario where we have a simple messaging system consisting of a producer, a queue, and a consumer. The producer generates messages, and the consumer processes them.

  - **Creating a queue:** To create a queue in RabbitMQ, you need to specify a name. For example, let us create a queue called "my_queue".

  - **Sending messages to the queue:** The producer sends messages to the queue by publishing them to an exchange. An exchange is responsible for routing messages to the appropriate queues based on specific rules. In our example, the producer sends messages to an exchange called "my_exchange".

  - **Storing messages in the queue:** When the producer publishes a message to the exchange, RabbitMQ routes the message to the specified queue ("my_queue" in our case). The queue then stores the message until a consumer consumes it. Messages are stored in the order they are received, forming a queue of messages.
  - **Consuming messages from the queue:** The consumer retrieves messages from the queue and processes them. Depending on the application's design, it can be a single or multiple consumer. When a consumer retrieves a message from the queue, it is considered "consumed" and removed from the queue.

- **Message acknowledgment:** After a consumer successfully processes a message, it acknowledges it to RabbitMQ. This acknowledgment informs RabbitMQ that the message has been successfully consumed and can be removed from the queue. If a consumer fails to acknowledge a message, RabbitMQ assumes it was not processed correctly and can re-queue it for another consumer to process.

  For example, let us consider a scenario where a producer sends three messages ("Message 1", "Message 2", "Message 3") to the "my_queue" in RabbitMQ. The messages are stored in the queue in the order they were published.

  The consumer, actively listening to the "my_queue", retrieves the messages from the queue individually. It consumes "Message 1", processes it, acknowledges the successful processing to RabbitMQ, and removes it from the queue. The consumer then consumes and processes "Message 2" and "Message 3" similarly.

  By utilizing queues, messages are stored until they can be processed by consumers, enabling asynchronous communication, and decoupling the producer from the consumer. Queues are critical in delivering messages and ensuring reliable and efficient communication in RabbitMQ-based systems.

- **Bindings in RabbitMQ:** In RabbitMQ, bindings are connections or associations between exchanges and queues. They define the rules for message routing and determine how messages flow from exchanges to queues.

Let us explore the concept of bindings in more detail with an example:

- o **Establishing bindings**: You need an exchange, a queue, and a routing key or pattern to establish a binding. The exchange is the source from which messages originate, the queue is the destination where messages are delivered, and the routing key or pattern specifies the conditions for routing messages.

  For example: Let us consider a scenario where we have a direct exchange named "my_direct_exchange" and a queue named "my_queue". We will create a binding between these two entities.

- o **Routing keys and patterns:** Routing keys or patterns determine how messages are matched and routed from the exchange to the queue. The routing key is a string associated with each message, and exchanges use it to determine which queues should receive the message. The routing key can be any string value the producer sets when publishing a message.

  For example, in our scenario, we can define routing keys such as "info", "error", or "warning". These routing keys represent different types or categories of messages.

- o **Direct exchange binding:** In a direct exchange, the binding between the exchange and the queue is based on the exact matching of the routing key. Each binding is associated with a specific routing key. When a message is published with a particular routing key, the direct exchange checks the bindings and routes the message to the queue with the matching routing key.

  For example, to create a binding between the "my_direct_exchange" and "my_queue", we specify a routing key, such as "info". This means messages with the routing key "info" will be delivered to the "my_queue".

- o **Topic exchange binding:** In a topic exchange, the binding between the exchange and the queue is based on patterns defined by the routing key. The routing key is a string composed of words separated by dots. The patterns can include wildcard characters:

- "*" matches a single word.
- "#" matches zero or more words.

For example, we have a topic exchange named "my_topic_exchange" and two queues, "queue1" and "queue2". We can create bindings with routing key patterns. For example, "queue1" can be bound with a routing key pattern of "error.#", and "queue2" can be bound with a pattern of "warning.*". Messages with routing keys like "error.system" or "error.network" will match the binding of "queue1", while messages with routing keys like "warning.log" or "warning.info" will match the binding of "queue2".

By creating bindings, you define the rules for message routing in RabbitMQ. Messages published to exchanges are distributed to queues based on these bindings, ensuring messages reach the intended destinations. Bindings are crucial in building flexible and efficient messaging systems, allowing for complex routing scenarios and enabling decoupling between producers and consumers.

.NET's relevance to event-driven systems

NET is a robust and versatile framework developed by Microsoft for building various applications, ranging from web applications to desktop software and even mobile apps. It provides a rich set of tools, libraries, and languages, with C# being one of the primary languages used for .NET development. One of the powerful capabilities of .NET is its ability to facilitate the creation of event-driven systems.

Event-driven systems are architectures where events drive the flow and execution of the application. Various sources, such as user interactions, sensor inputs, messages from external systems, or internal state changes, can trigger events. Using the event-driven approach, applications can respond to events asynchronously and reactively, enabling them to be more flexible, modular, and scalable.

.NET offers several features and components that make it well-suited for developing event-driven systems:

- **Event model**: .NET provides a robust event model that allows developers to define, publish, and subscribe to events within their applications. The event model is based on delegates, which are objects that hold references to methods. Delegates enable the decoupling of event publishers from event subscribers, allowing for loose coupling and modularity.

- **Delegates and event handlers**: In .NET, delegates act as the bridge between event publishers and subscribers. They define the signature of the methods that can be invoked in response to an event. Event handlers are methods associated with specific events and executed when the event is raised. Delegates and event handlers facilitate communication between components in an event-driven system.
- **Event publishing**: .NET lets developers define and publish events within their classes. Events can be declared using the event keyword and are typically accompanied by an event handler delegate. By raising an event, publishers notify subscribers of a specific event, triggering the execution of the associated event handlers.
- **Event subscribing**: Subscribing to events allows components to listen and respond to specific events of interest. In .NET, event subscribers can register their event handlers with the publishers to receive notifications when the events are raised. This decoupled nature enables multiple subscribers to react to events independently.
- **Asynchronous programming**: .NET provides extensive support for asynchronous programming, which is crucial in event-driven systems. Asynchronous programming allows the application to continue processing events and executing tasks without waiting for each operation to complete, thus improving responsiveness and scalability.
- **Frameworks and libraries**: The .NET ecosystem offers various frameworks and libraries that facilitate event-driven development. For instance, **Windows Presentation Foundation (WPF)** and Windows Forms provide built-in event mechanisms for handling user interface events. Additionally, frameworks like Azure Service Bus and RabbitMQ offer messaging capabilities that facilitate event-driven communication between distributed components.

- **Testing and debugging**: .NET provides robust testing and debugging tools to aid in developing event-driven systems. Developers can leverage these tools to simulate events, monitor event flows, and diagnose issues related to event handling and execution.

  By harnessing the features and capabilities of .NET, developers can build event-driven systems that are highly responsive, modular, and scalable. The event-driven architecture provided by .NET empowers applications to efficiently handle various events and deliver a seamless user experience.

RabbitMQ implementation for building event-driven .NET applications

This section will outline the steps involved in preparing your system for the implementation of event-driven systems.

Installing RabbitMQ server

RabbitMQ Server is an open-source message broker software that implements the **Advanced Message Queuing Protocol (AMQP)**. It provides a reliable and scalable messaging system for building distributed applications and facilitates communication between different components or services.

At its core, RabbitMQ enables asynchronous and decoupled communication between producers and consumers. Producers are responsible for sending messages (events) to RabbitMQ, while consumers receive and process these messages. The messages are typically organized into queues, ensuring that they are stored until the intended recipients consume them.

Follow these steps to configure your .NET IDE for event-driven architecture with RabbitMQ:

1. Download the supported version of **Erlang** for Windows. It is recommended to install a 64-bit version. Refer to the following figure:

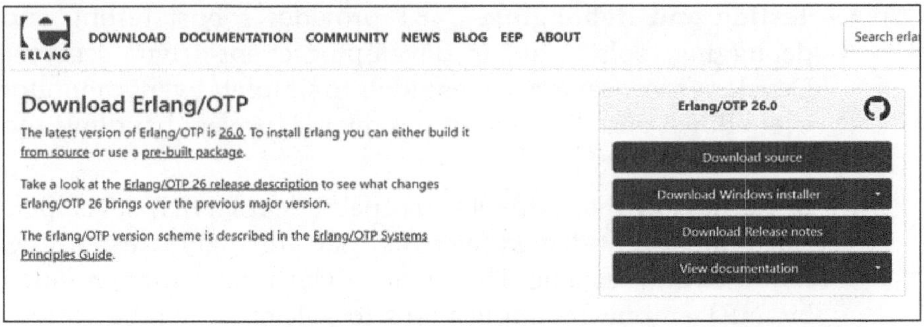

Figure 4.2: *Erlang Installation*

2. Let us install the downloaded exe file with the default configuration. Make sure that the Erlang installer runs with an admin account.
3. **Download and Install RabbitMQ Server from:**

   https://www.rabbitmq.com/install-windows.html# installer

   Refer to the following figure:

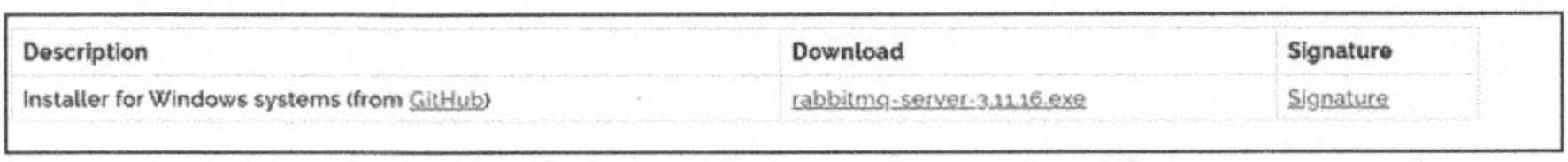

Description	Download	Signature
Installer for Windows systems (from GitHub)	rabbitmq-server-3.11.16.exe	Signature

Figure 4.3: *RabbitMQ Server Window Installer*

4. Let us install the downloaded exe file with the default configuration.

Note: We would get a warning if we did not install Erlang first as per the previous step. Refer to the following figure:

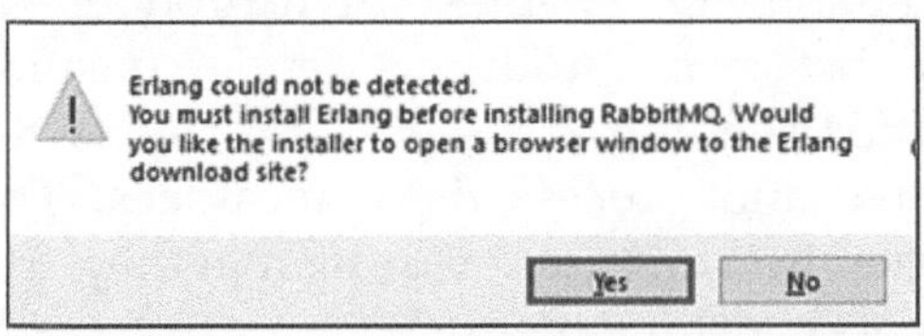

Figure 4.4: *RabbitMQ Server Window Installer*

5. **Enable RabbitMQ Management from CMD.** Let us open Command Prompt, then go to **`cd C:\Program Files\RabbitMQ Server\rabbitmq_server-3.11.16\sbin`**:

   `rabbitmq-plugins.bat enable rabbitmq_management`

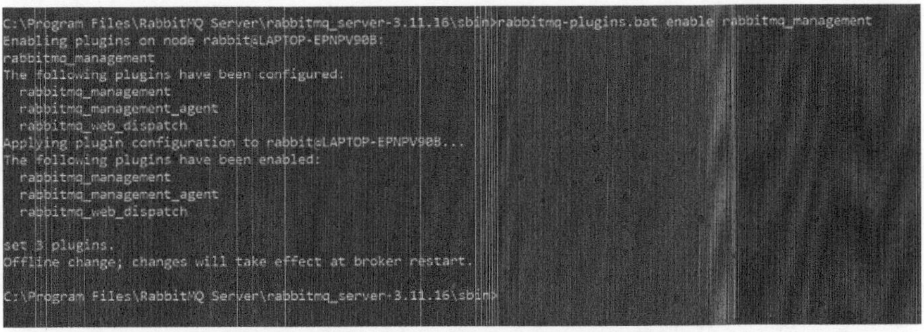

***Figure 4.5:** Enable RabbitMQ Management*

6. Now let is browse and log in to the RabbitMQ server. Let us open this URL in the browser **`http://localhost:15672/#/`** and log in with the username and password **guest**:

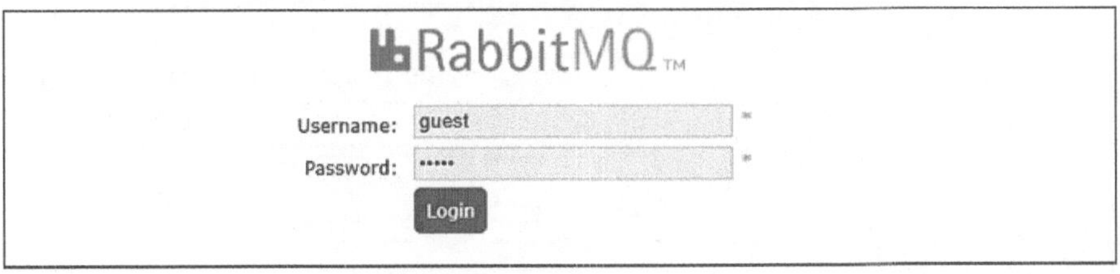

***Figure 4.6:** RabbitMQ Login Screen*

7. Once you have successfully logged in, the RabbitMQ dashboard will automatically open. Refer to the following figure:

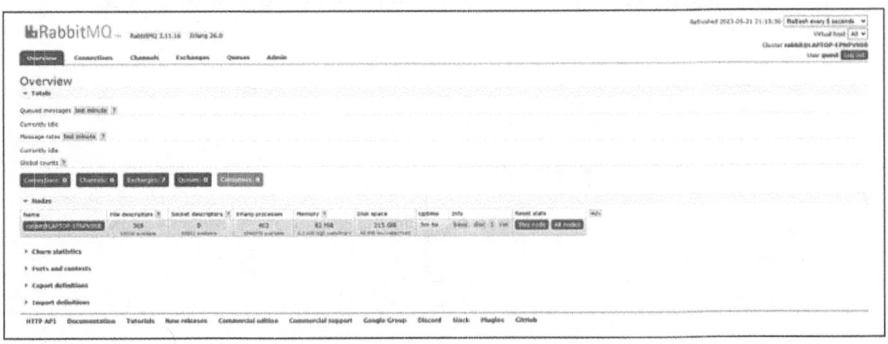

***Figure 4.7:** RabbitMQ Dashboard*

RabbitMQ is now up and running on your local host. You have successfully set up the RabbitMQ server, which will serve as the messaging backbone for your event-driven system. You can start building and integrating your components using RabbitMQ for asynchronous and decoupled communication.

Setting up a .NET project for event-driven architecture

To prepare the system, we can start by creating a new project and adding the RabbitMQ client to it.

1. We will create a .NET Publisher API for our project. Create a new .NET project in Visual Studio, as shown in the following figure:

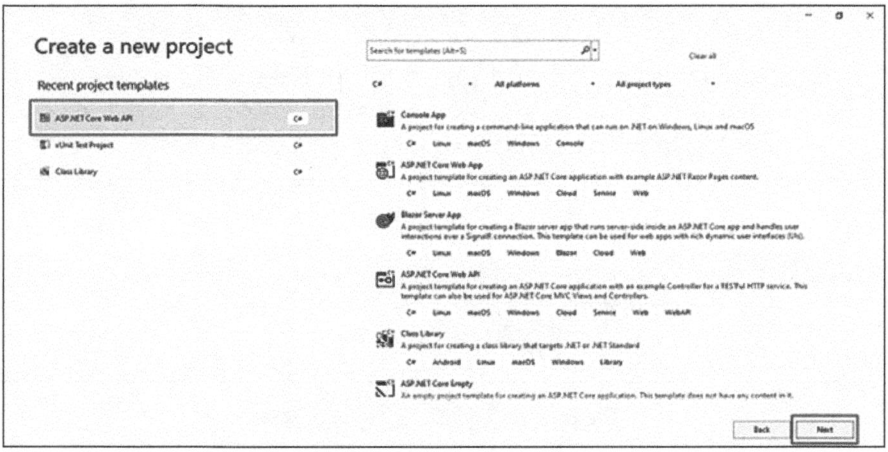

Figure 4.8: *.NET Project Creation*

2. Configure your project as shown in the following figure:

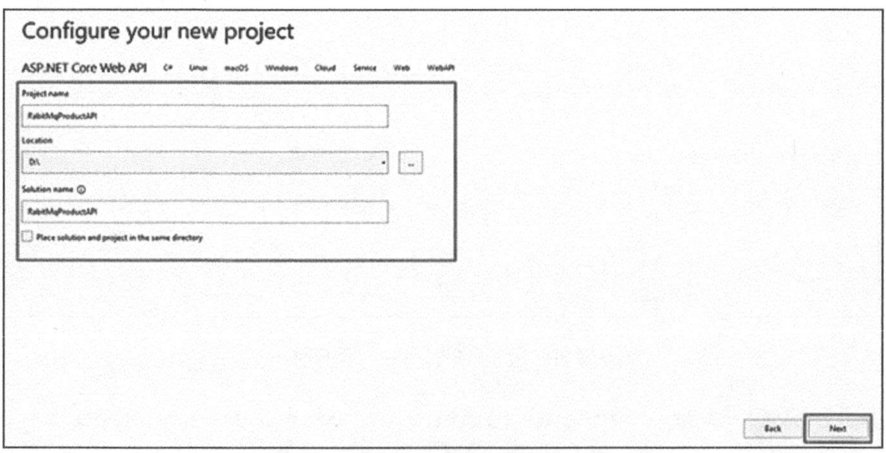

Figure 4.9: *Publisher API*

3. Provide **Additional information** as shown in the following figure:

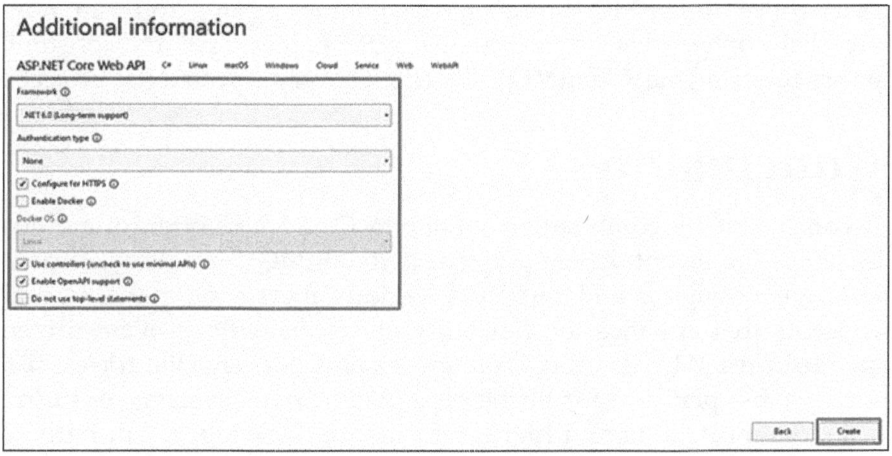

Figure 4.10: Publisher API Configuration

4. Right-click on your project in the **Solution Explorer** and select **Manage NuGet Packages**.

   In the NuGet Package Manager, search for **RabbitMQ.Client**. Select the **RabbitMQ. Client** package and click **Install** to add it to your project, as shown in the following figure:

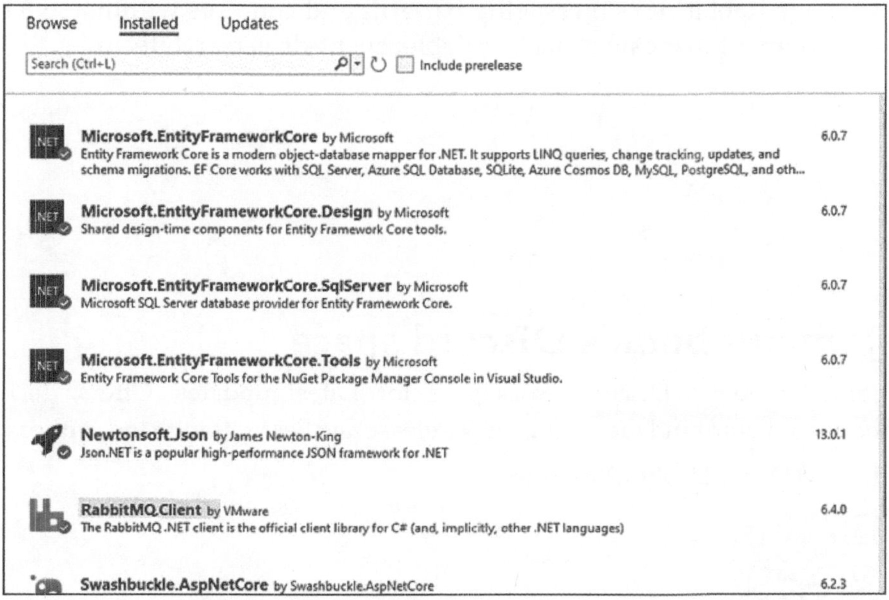

Figure 4.11: Rabbit MQ Client Package Addition

After installing both the RabbitMQ .NET client and the RabbitMQ Server, you have the necessary components to develop applications that utilize RabbitMQ for event-driven messaging. You can now establish connections, declare queues, publish messages, and consume messages using the RabbitMQ .NET client library in your .NET projects.

Conclusion

In conclusion, the combination of RabbitMQ and .NET offers numerous benefits for event-driven systems. RabbitMQ provides efficient message queueing and supports various messaging patterns and concepts that enhance the flexibility and scalability of event-driven architectures. With its robust framework and extensive libraries, .NET is a suitable platform for developing event-driven systems, ensuring seamless integration and high performance. Developers can harness the full potential of event-driven systems and build robust, scalable applications by properly setting up a .NET project for event-driven architecture and leveraging RabbitMQ's messaging capabilities.

The next chapter delves into the practical implementation of event-driven systems using RabbitMQ and .NET. It provides step-by-step instructions, code examples, and best practices for building event publishers, subscribers, and handlers. It demonstrates how to leverage RabbitMQ's messaging patterns and concepts within a .NET environment to create robust, scalable, event-driven architectures.

CHAPTER 5

Building Event-Driven System with RabbitMQ and .NET

Introduction

Building an Event-Driven System with RabbitMQ and .NET will explore the practical implementation of developing event-driven systems. It will give an in-depth understanding of the features and capabilities of RabbitMQ and .NET for building event-driven systems. This implementation will teach you how to set up an Event-Driven System Project in .NET using RabbitMQ libraries.

Structure

In this chapter, we will cover the following topics:

- Setting up RabbitMQ as messaging broker
- Implementing event producers using .NET
- Implementing event consumers using .NET
- Error handling techniques for RabbitMQ event publishing
- Reliable message delivery using RabbitMQ's

Objectives

This chapter provides comprehensive coverage of setting up RabbitMQ as a messaging broker, including installation, configuration, and defining message queues and exchanges. It also explores the implementation of event producers in .NET for generating and publishing events, along with building event consumers in .NET to subscribe to event queues and process incoming events. Additionally, the chapter delves into error-handling techniques like retry mechanisms, testing strategies such as unit testing, monitoring, and logging techniques for real-time event analysis, and deployment options involving local environments or cloud services like Azure or AWS, addressing service discovery and load balancing considerations.

Setting up RabbitMQ as messaging broker

In *Chapter 4, Implementing Event-driven Architecture with RabbitMQ and .NET*, we explored the installation and configuration process of RabbitMQ as a message broker. In this chapter, we will learn how to define message queues and exchanges using practical examples to expand our understanding of RabbitMQ's capabilities. Below are the steps to set up RabbitMQ:

1. The RabbitMQ service starts automatically. You can stop | reinstall | and start the RabbitMQ service from the Start Menu. Refer to the following figure:

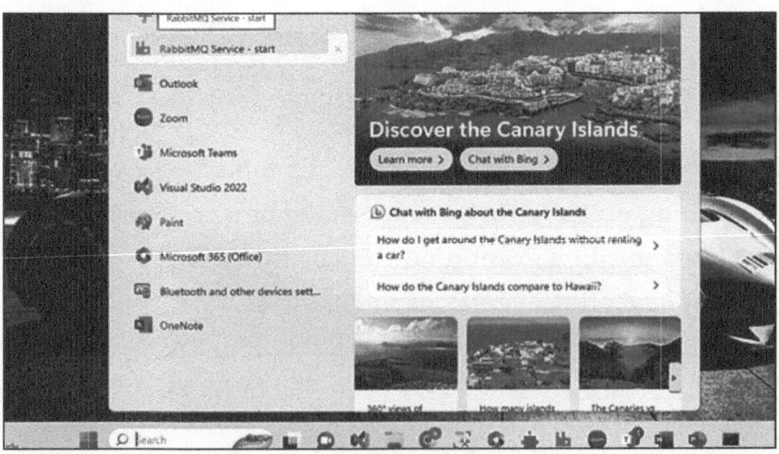

Figure 5.1: *Starting RabbitMQ Service*

2. Step 2. After restarting the RabbitMQ service, browse **http://localhost:15672/** to open the RabbitMQ management and log in using guest as Username and Password, as shown in the following figure:

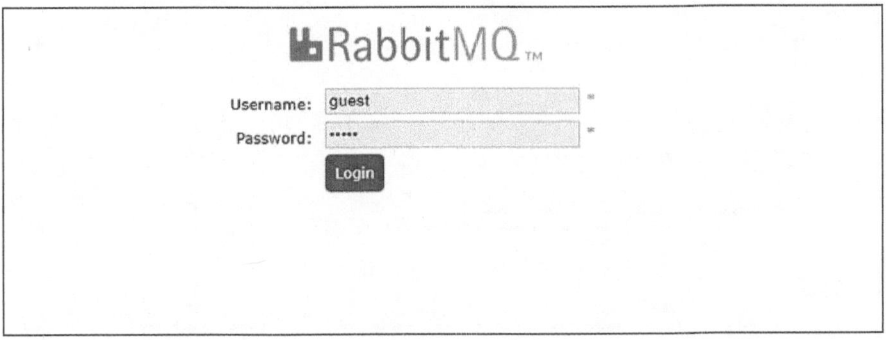

***Figure 5.2:** RabbitMQ Management Console*

3. In the RabbitMQ management console, navigate to the **Queues** tab, as shown in *Figure 5.3*:

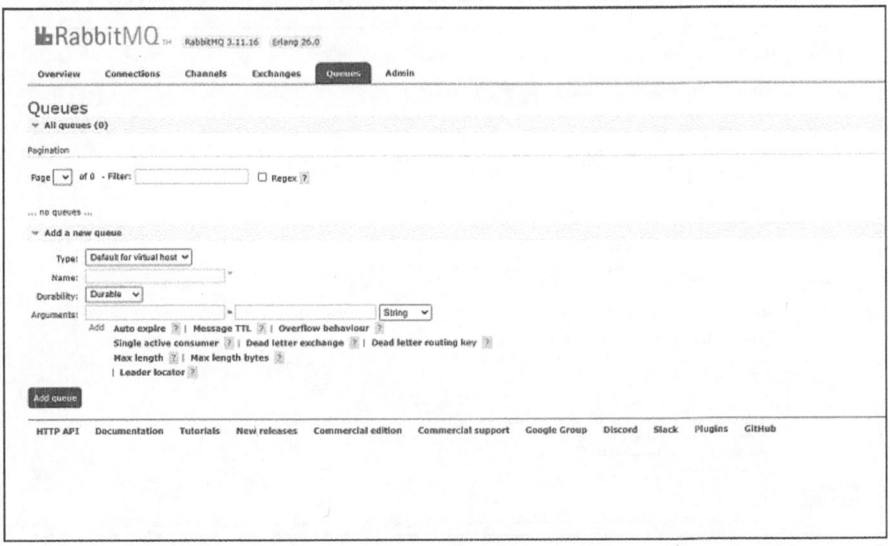

***Figure 5.3:** Queues tab in RabbitMQ Management Console*

4. Click on the Add a new queue button to create a new queue. Provide a name for the queue (For example, myQueue) and click **Add queue**, as shown in the following figure:

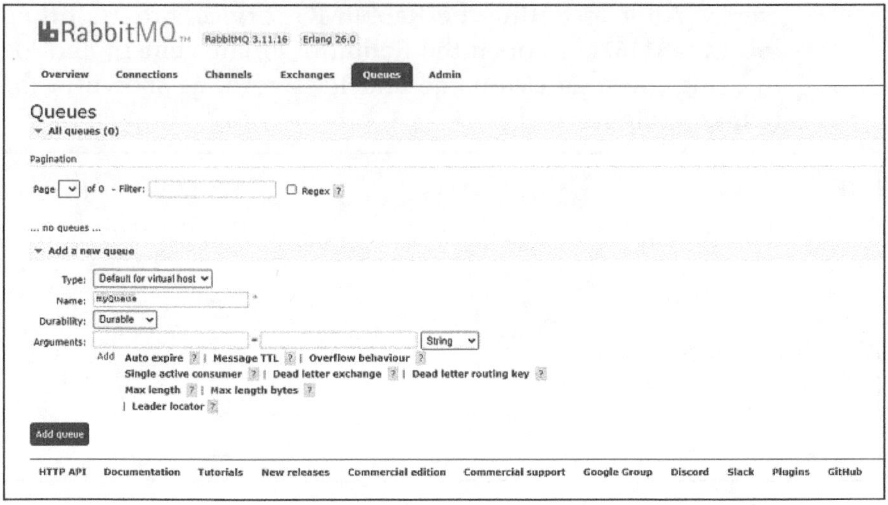

Figure 5.4: Adding Queue Name

5. Make sure to verify that you can locate the newly created queue **myQueue** within the list of queues. Refer to *Figure 5.5:*

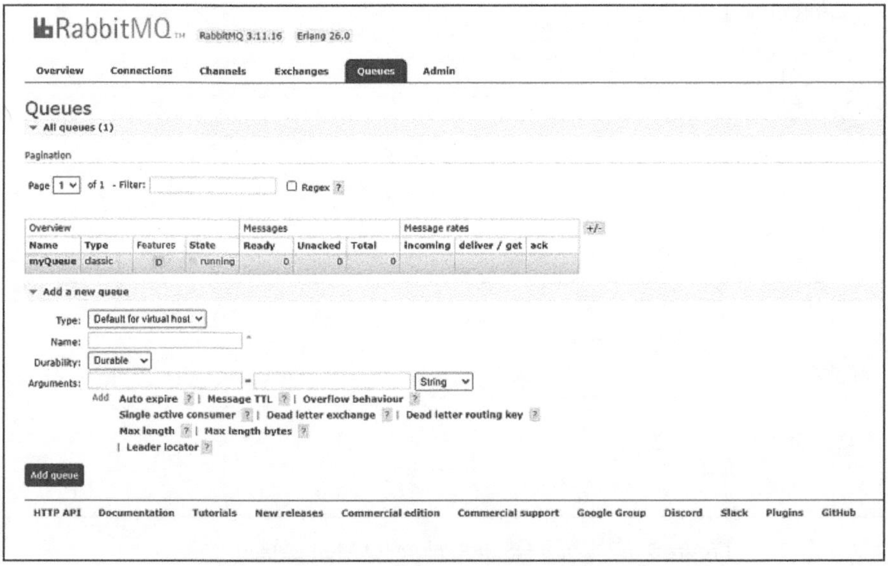

Figure 5.5: Verifying Queue Creation

6. In the RabbitMQ management console, navigate to the **Exchanges** tab, as shown in *Figure 5.6*:

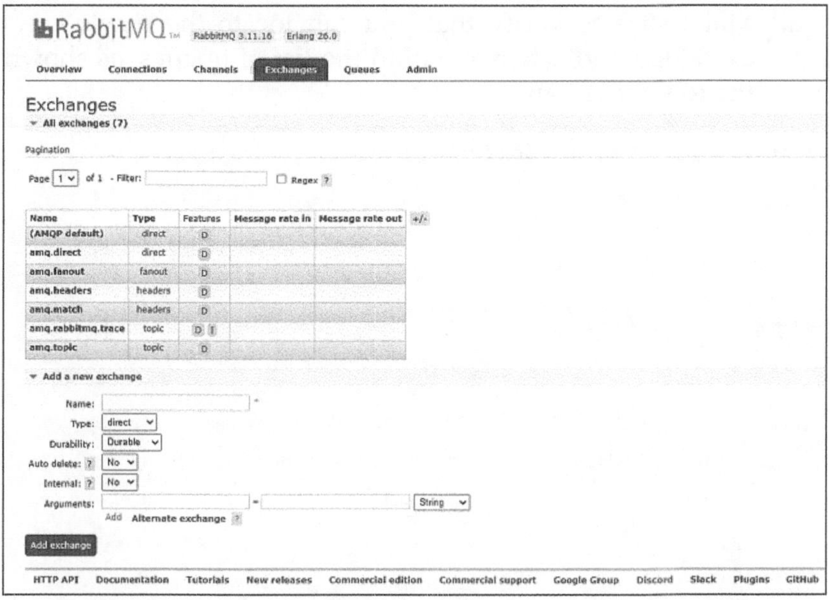

***Figure 5.6:** Exchanges tab in RabbitMQ Management Console*

7. Click on **Add a new exchange**. Choose the desired exchange type (For example, direct, fanout, topic) and provide a name for the exchange (For example, myExchange). Click **Add exchange** to create it. Refer to the following figure:

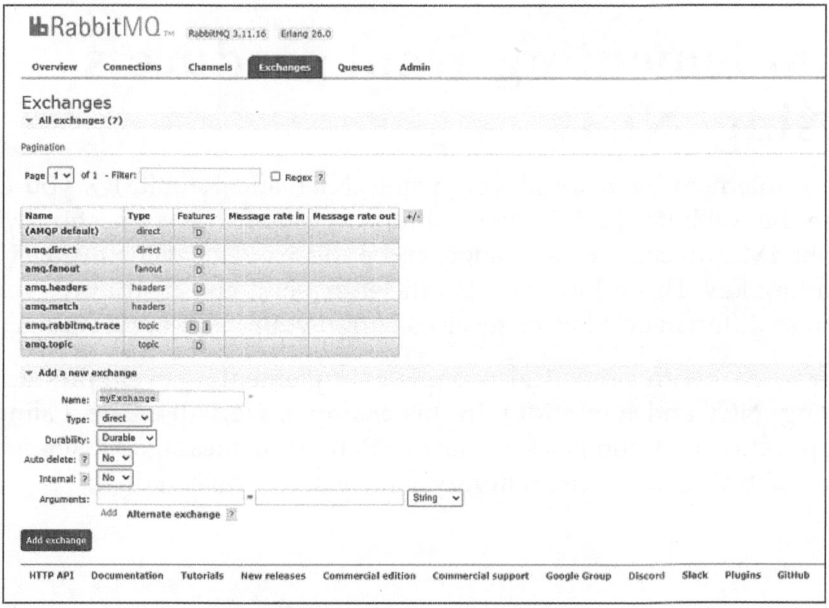

***Figure 5.7:** Adding Exchange Name*

8. Make sure to verify that you can locate the newly created exchange myExchange within the list of queues, as shown in the following figure:

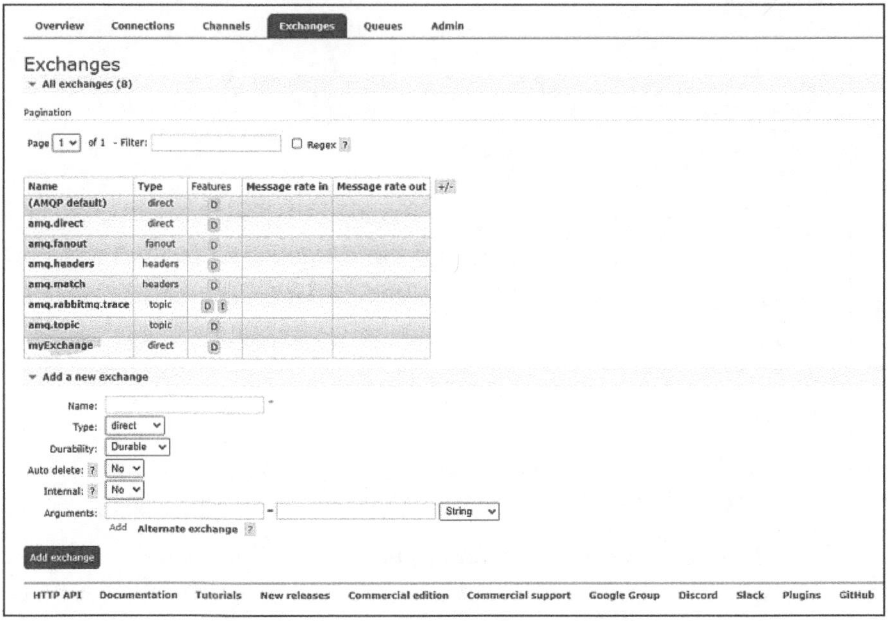

Figure 5.8: Verifying Exchange Creation

Implementing event producers using .NET

To implement event producers using .NET and RabbitMQ, you can use the RabbitMQ .NET client library to establish a connection with RabbitMQ, declare the exchange, and publish events using the desired routing key. This allows you to efficiently send and distribute events across different systems or services within your .NET applications.

Let us start with a practical example of implementing event producers using .NET and RabbitMQ. In this example, we will create a simple application that publishes events to a RabbitMQ message broker using the RabbitMQ .NET client library. Here is how you can do it:

1. Create a new .NET project using your preferred IDE. You can choose a Console Application, as shown in the following figure:

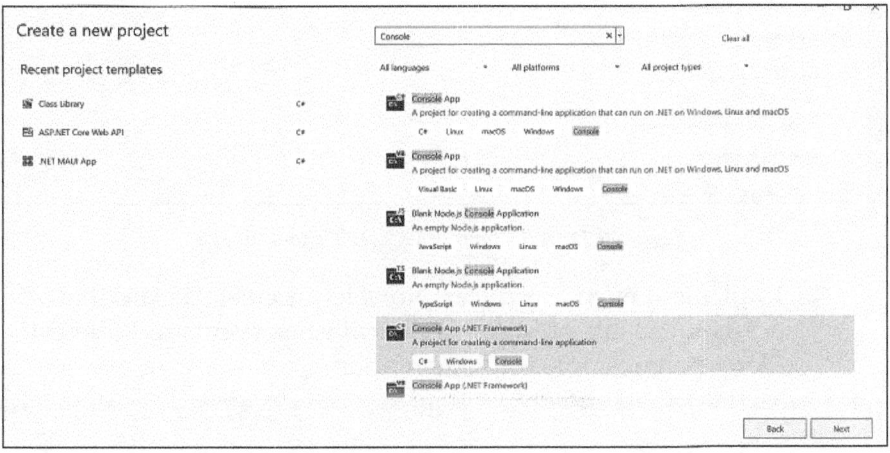

Figure 5.9: Create .NET Project in Visual Studio

2. Configure a new project and give it a specific project name. Refer to *Figure 5.10*:

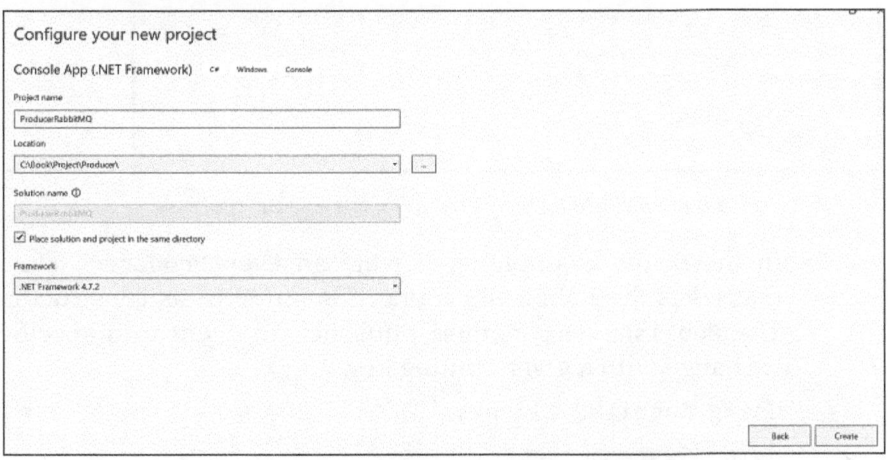

Figure 5.10: Configure Project using Project Name

3. Add RabbitMQ .NET client library using Manage Nuget Package Manager, as shown in the following figure:

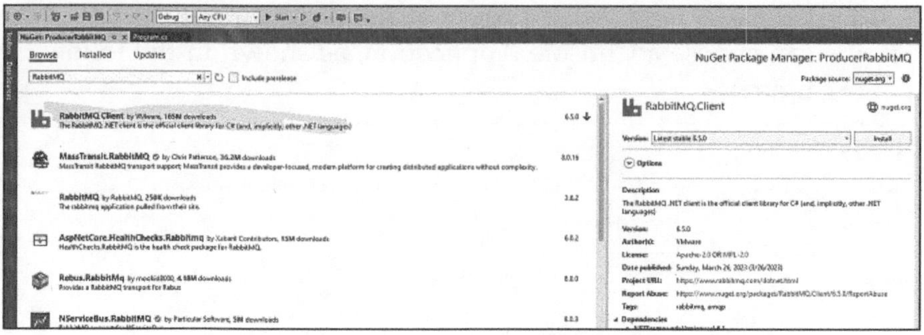

***Figure 5.11**: Add RammitMQ.NET client library*

4. Implement event producer. Now, let us create a class that will act as the event producer and publishes events to RabbitMQ. Here is an example implementation:

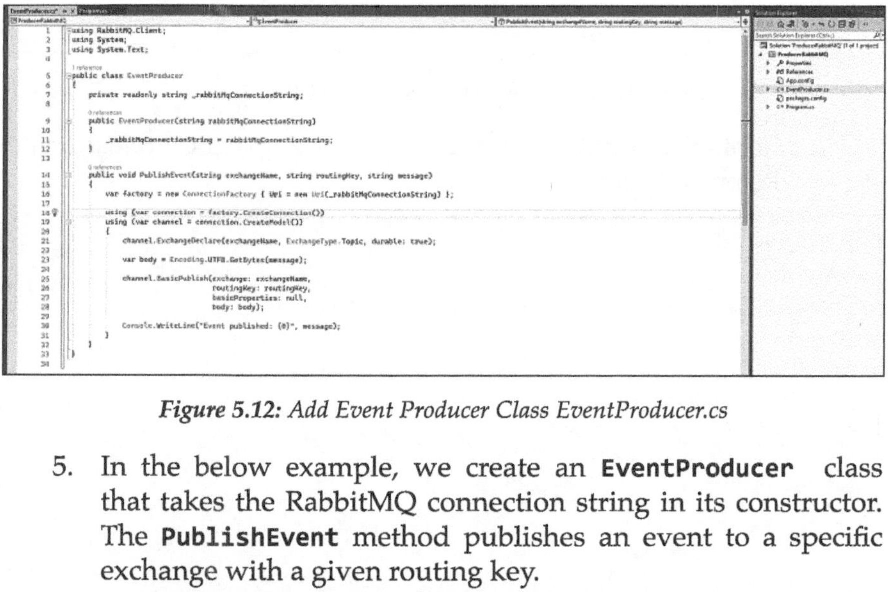

***Figure 5.12:** Add Event Producer Class EventProducer.cs*

5. In the below example, we create an **`EventProducer`** class that takes the RabbitMQ connection string in its constructor. The **`PublishEvent`** method publishes an event to a specific exchange with a given routing key.

```
using RabbitMQ.Client;
using System;
using System.Text;

public class EventProducer
{
    private readonly string _rabbitMqConnectionString;
```

```
    public EventProducer(string rabbitMqConnection-
    String)
    {
        _rabbitMqConnectionString = rabbitMqConnec-
        tionString;
    }

    public void PublishEvent(string exchangeName,
    string routingKey, string message)
    {
        var factory = new ConnectionFactory { Uri =
        new Uri(_rabbitMqConnectionString) };

        using (var connection = factory.CreateCon-
        nection())
       using (var channel = connection.CreateModel())
        {
            channel.ExchangeDeclare(exchangeName,
            ExchangeType.Topic, durable: true);

          var body = Encoding.UTF8.GetBytes(message);

         channel.BasicPublish(exchange: exchangeName,
                                routingKey: routingKey,
                                 basicProperties: null,
                                    body: body);

            Console.WriteLine("Event published:
            {0}", message);
        }
    }
}
```

6. **Publish events**: Now, you can use the **EventProducer** class to publish events from your application. Here is an example of how you can use it:

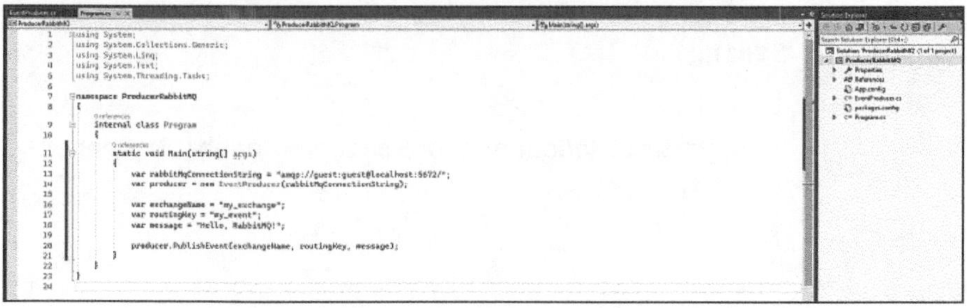

***Figure 5.13:** Add program class to invoke publish event method*

7. Refer to the below code for implementation detail about invoking **`PublishEvent`** method:

```
namespace ProducerRabbitMQ
{
    internal class Program
    {
        static void Main(string[] args)
        {
            var rabbitMqConnectionString = "amqp://
            guest:guest@localhost:5672/";
            var producer = new EventProducer(rabbit-
            MqConnectionString);

            var exchangeName = "my_exchange";
            var routingKey = "my_event";
            var message = "Hello, RabbitMQ!";

            producer.PublishEvent(exchangeName,
            routingKey, message);
        }
    }
}
```

Implementing event consumers using .NET

Event consumers are components responsible for receiving and processing events from a message broker like RabbitMQ. In the context of .NET applications, event consumers can be implemented using the RabbitMQ .NET client library, which provides the necessary functionality to establish a connection with RabbitMQ and receive messages.

To implement an event consumer in .NET with RabbitMQ, you will need to follow these steps:

1. **Create a .NET project**: Begin by creating a new .NET project in your preferred IDE. Choose the appropriate project template based on the type of application you are building. For example, you can use a Console Application, Web API, or any other suitable template.

2. **Add RabbitMQ .NET client library**: To interact with RabbitMQ from your .NET application, you will need to add the RabbitMQ .NET client library as a dependency. This library provides classes and methods for establishing connections, declaring exchanges and queues, and receiving messages. You can add the RabbitMQ .NET client library to your project by using the NuGet package manager. Refer to *Step 2 of Implementing event producers using .NET*.

3. **Implement the event consumer**: Create a class that will act as the event consumer and receives events from RabbitMQ. This class will typically have a method to start consuming events. Here is an example implementation:

```
using RabbitMQ.Client;
using RabbitMQ.Client.Events;
using System;
using System.Text;

public class EventConsumer
{
    private readonly string rabbitMqConnectionString;
```

```
public EventConsumer(string rabbitMqConnection-
String)
{
    this.rabbitMqConnectionString = rabbitMqCon-
    nectionString;
}

public void ConsumeEvents(string exchangeName,
string queueName, string routingKey)
{
    var factory = new ConnectionFactory { Uri =
    new Uri(rabbitMqConnectionString) };

    using (var connection = factory.
    CreateConnection())
   using (var channel = connection.CreateModel())
    {
        channel.ExchangeDeclare(exchangeName,
        ExchangeType.Topic);
        channel.QueueDeclare(queueName, durable:
        true, exclusive: false, autoDelete:
        false);
        channel.QueueBind(queueName,
        exchangeName, routingKey);

        var consumer = new EventingBasicConsum-
        er(channel);
        consumer.Received += (model, ea) =>
        {
            var body = ea.Body.ToArray();
            var message = Encoding.UTF8.
            GetString(body);
            Console.WriteLine("Event received:
            {0}", message);
        };
```

```
                    channel.BasicConsume(queueName, autoAck:
                    true, consumer: consumer);

                    Console.WriteLine("Waiting for events.
                    Press any key to exit.");
                    Console.ReadLine();
                }
            }
        }
```

4. In this example, we create an **EventConsumer** class that takes the RabbitMQ connection string in its constructor. The **ConsumeEvents** method sets up the exchange, queue, and binding and starts consuming events from the specified queue. When an event is received, it prints the message to the console.

5. Use the event consumer: You can now use the **EventConsumer** class to consume events in your application. Here is an example of how you can use it:

```
static void Main(string[] args)
{
    var rabbitMqConnectionString = "amqp://
    guest:guest@localhost:5672/";
    var consumer = new
    EventConsumer(rabbitMqConnectionString);

    var exchangeName = "my_exchange";
    var queueName = "my_queue";
    var routingKey = "my_event";

    consumer.ConsumeEvents(exchangeName, queueName,
    routingKey);
}
```

6. **ConsumeEvents** In this example, we create an instance of the **EventConsumer** class and call the method to start consuming events from the **"my_queue"** queue, which is bound to the **"my_exchange"** exchange with the **"my_event"** routing key.

7. Remember to replace the RabbitMQ connection string, exchange name, queue name, and routing key with your actual values.

You have now successfully implemented an event consumer using .NET and RabbitMQ.

Error handling techniques for RabbitMQ event publishing

Handling failures when producing or consuming events is crucial for ensuring message delivery and maintaining reliability in event-driven systems. Here are some error-handling techniques and retry mechanisms that you can employ:

- **Retry mechanisms**: These are used to handle failures and retries when producing or consuming events in .NET applications with RabbitMQ. They allow you to automatically retry failed operations, ensuring message delivery and improving the reliability of your event-driven system.

  Here is a simple example of implementing a retry mechanism in .NET with RabbitMQ:

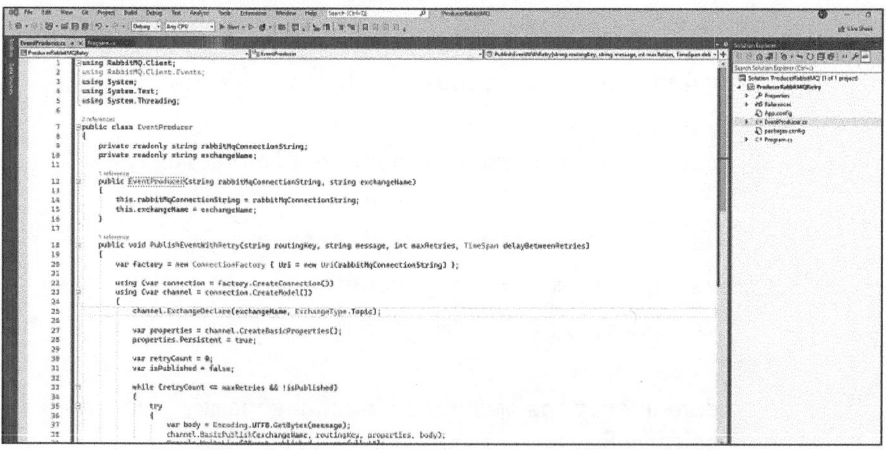

Figure 5.14: *Add event producer class EventProducer*

  In the below example, we have an **`EventProducer`** class that takes the RabbitMQ connection string and exchanges the name in its constructor. The **`PublishEventWithRetry`** method publishes an event to RabbitMQ using the specified routing key and message.

```
using RabbitMQ.Client;
using RabbitMQ.Client.Events;
using System;
using System.Text;
using System.Threading;

public class EventProducer
{
    private readonly string rabbitMqConnectionString;
    private readonly string exchangeName;

    public EventProducer(string rabbitMqConnection-
    String, string exchangeName)
    {
        this.rabbitMqConnectionString = rabbitMqCon-
        nectionString;
        this.exchangeName = exchangeName;
    }

    public void PublishEventWithRetry(string
    routingKey, string message, int maxRetries,
    TimeSpan delayBetweenRetries)
    {
        var factory = new ConnectionFactory { Uri =
        new Uri(rabbitMqConnectionString) };

        using (var connection = factory.CreateCon-
        nection())
        using (var channel = connection.CreateMod-
        el())
        {
            channel.ExchangeDeclare(exchangeName,
            ExchangeType.Topic);

            var properties = channel.CreateBa-
            sicProperties();
```

```
            properties.Persistent = true;

            var retryCount = 0;
            var isPublished = false;

            while (retryCount <= maxRetries &&
            !isPublished)
            {
                try
                {
                    var body = Encoding.UTF8.Get-
                    Bytes(message);
                    channel.
                    BasicPublish(exchangeName,
                    routingKey, properties, body);
                    Console.WriteLine("Event
                    published successfully!");
                    isPublished = true;
                }
                catch (Exception ex)
                {
                    Console.WriteLine($"Failed to
                    publish event: {ex.Message}");
                    retryCount++;
                  Thread.Sleep(delayBetweenRetries);
                }
            }

            if (!isPublished)
            {
                Console.WriteLine("Failed to publish
                event after maximum retries.");

            }
        }
```

```
        }
    }
```

The retry mechanism is implemented using a while loop. The loop continues until either the event is successfully published or the maximum number of retries is reached. If an exception occurs during publishing, the exception is caught, the retry count is incremented, and the process waits for a specified delay before the next retry.

Here is a simple example of implementing an Event Producer mechanism in .NET with RabbitMQ:

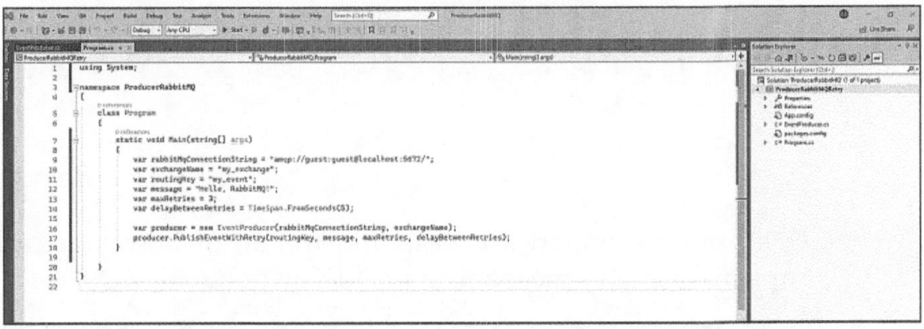

Figure 5.15: Add Program Class to invoke PublishEventWithRetry method

In the below example, we create an instance of the **EventProducer** class and call the **PublishEventWithRetry** method to publish an event with retry. If the event fails to be published, it will retry up to **maxRetries** times with a delay of **delayBetweenRetries** between each retry.

```
using System;

namespace ProducerRabbitMQ
{
    class Program
    {
        static void Main(string[] args)
        {
            var rabbitMqConnectionString = "amqp://
            guest:guest@localhost:5672/";
            var exchangeName = "my_exchange";
```

```
                var routingKey = "my_event";
                var message = "Hello, RabbitMQ!";
                var maxRetries = 3;
                var delayBetweenRetries = TimeSpan.From-
                Seconds(5);

                var producer = new EventProducer(rabbit-
                MqConnectionString, exchangeName);
                producer.PublishEventWithRetry(rout-
                ingKey, message, maxRetries, delayBe-
                tweenRetries);
            }

        }
    }
```

This example provides a basic illustration of how you can implement a retry mechanism in .NET with RabbitMQ.

- **Dead letter Queues (DLQ)**: DLQs are special queues in RabbitMQ used to handle messages that cannot be delivered to their intended destination or have failed to process. DLQs provide a mechanism for capturing and storing messages that encounter errors or exceptional conditions during publishing or consumption. Messages typically end up in a DLQ due to reasons like expired time-to-live, rejected by consumers, or reaching maximum retry attempts. DLQs allow for manual inspection, analysis, and handling of failed messages, enabling appropriate actions to be taken.

Steps to implement DLQ in RabbitMQ:

1. **To set up a Dead Letter Queue in RabbitMQ, you need to define two components**: an exchange and a queue.
2. **Create a Dead Letter Exchange**: This exchange captures failed messages and routes them to the Dead Letter Queue. Specify the type of exchange (e.g., direct, topic) based on your requirements.
3. **Create a Dead Letter Queue**: This queue acts as the destination for failed messages. Configure the queue to bind to the Dead Letter Exchange and specify any additional parameters (e.g., message TTL, maximum retry attempts).

4. **Bind the Original Queue to the Dead Letter Exchange**: Specify the routing key or binding pattern for the original queue to route failed messages to the Dead Letter Exchange.

   Here is an example of implementing DLQ in .NET with RabbitMQ:

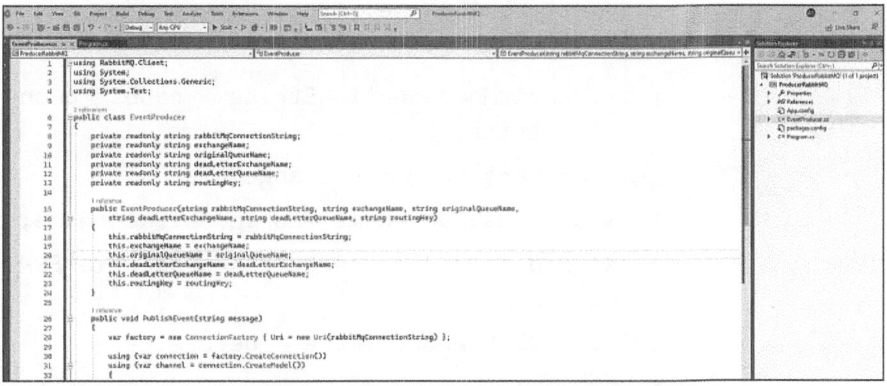

Figure 5.16: *Add Event Producer Class EventProducer*

5. In the below example, we have an **EventProducer** class that takes the RabbitMQ connection string, exchange name, original queue name, dead letter exchange name, dead letter queue name, and routing key in its constructor. The **PublishEvent** method publishes an event message to RabbitMQ using the specified exchange and routing key.

```
using RabbitMQ.Client;
using System;
using System.Collections.Generic;
using System.Text;

public class EventProducer
{
    private readonly string rabbitMqConnectionString;
    private readonly string exchangeName;
    private readonly string originalQueueName;
    private readonly string deadLetterExchangeName;
    private readonly string deadLetterQueueName;
    private readonly string routingKey;
```

```
public EventProducer(string rabbitMqConnection-
String, string exchangeName, string original-
QueueName,
    string deadLetterExchangeName, string
    deadLetterQueueName, string routingKey)
{
    this.rabbitMqConnectionString = rabbitMqCon-
    nectionString;
    this.exchangeName = exchangeName;
    this.originalQueueName = originalQueueName;
    this.deadLetterExchangeName = deadLetterEx-
    changeName;
    this.deadLetterQueueName = deadLetter-
    QueueName;
    this.routingKey = routingKey;
}

public void PublishEvent(string message)
{
    var factory = new ConnectionFactory { Uri =
    new Uri(rabbitMqConnectionString) };

    using (var connection = factory.CreateCon-
    nection())
    using (var channel = connection.CreateMod-
    el())
    {
        // Declare the original queue with DLQ
        configuration
        channel.QueueDeclare(originalQueueName,
        durable: true, exclusive: false, autoDe-
        lete: false,
            arguments: new Dictionary<string,
            object>
```

```
                {
                    { "x-dead-letter-exchange",
                    deadLetterExchangeName },
                    { "x-dead-letter-routing-key",
                    routingKey }
                });

            // Declare the dead letter exchange and
            queue
            channel.
            ExchangeDeclare(deadLetterExchangeName,
            ExchangeType.Direct, durable: true);
            channel.QueueDeclare(deadLetter-
            QueueName, durable: true, exclusive:
            false, autoDelete: false, arguments:
            null);
            channel.QueueBind(deadLetterQueueName,
            deadLetterExchangeName, routingKey,
            null);

            var properties = channel.CreateBa-
            sicProperties();
            properties.Persistent = true;

            var body = Encoding.UTF8.GetBytes(mes-
            sage);
            channel.BasicPublish(exchangeName,
            routingKey, properties, body);

            Console.WriteLine("Event published
            successfully!");
        }
    }
}
```

6. To use the **EventProducer** with dead letter queues:

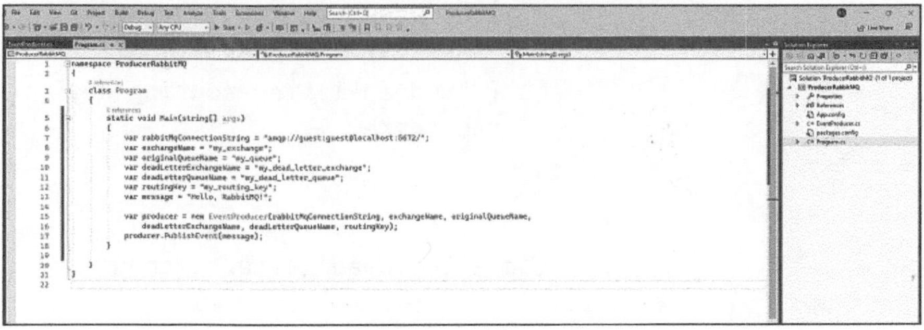

Figure 5.17: *Add Program Class to invoke PublishEvent method*

7. In the below example, we create an instance of the **EventProducer** class and call the **PublishEvent** method to publish an event message. If any errors occur during publishing or if the message is not consumed successfully, it will be routed to the dead letter queue defined by the **deadLetterExchangeName** and **deadLetterQueueName**:

```
namespace ProducerRabbitMQ
{
    class Program
    {
        static void Main(string[] args)
        {
            var rabbitMqConnectionString = "amqp://
            guest:guest@localhost:5672/";
            var exchangeName = "my_exchange";
            var originalQueueName = "my_queue";
            var deadLetterExchangeName = "my_dead_
            letter_exchange";
            var deadLetterQueueName = "my_dead_
            letter_queue";
            var routingKey = "my_routing_key";
            var message = "Hello, RabbitMQ!";

            var producer = new EventProducer(rabbit-
            MqConnectionString, exchangeName, origi-
            nalQueueName,
```

```
                    deadLetterExchangeName,
                    deadLetterQueueName, routingKey);
                producer.PublishEvent(message);
            }
        }
    }
```

- **Circuit breaker pattern**: It plays a crucial role in handling errors and failures between event producers and consumers. It helps protect the system from cascading failures and provides a more resilient and responsive environment for handling events.
- **Protecting event producers**: To ensure the reliability of event producers when sending events to RabbitMQ or other message brokers, the Circuit Breaker pattern can be utilized. By setting an error threshold, the Circuit Breaker detects excessive failures and suspends event transmission. This prevents overwhelming the message broker and allows it time to recover. During the open state, the event producer can handle failures by logging them or redirecting events to a dead-letter queue for further analysis.
- **Handling errors in event consumers**: When event consumers encounter errors during the processing of incoming events, the Circuit Breaker pattern can be employed to handle these failures and prevent cascading issues. If the error rate surpasses a predefined limit within a specific timeframe, the Circuit Breaker trips, blocking the faulty event from further processing. Instead, the Circuit Breaker can perform actions like logging the error, marking the event as failed, or invoking a fallback mechanism to gracefully handle the error and avoid system-wide disruptions.

To implement the Circuit Breaker pattern in .NET with RabbitMQ, you can use the Polly library, which provides robust resilience and transient-fault-handling capabilities. Here is an example that demonstrates how to use the Circuit Breaker pattern with a simple RabbitMQ producer:

1. First, make sure you have the Polly NuGet package installed in your project. You can install it using NuGet Package Manager (refer to the following figure):

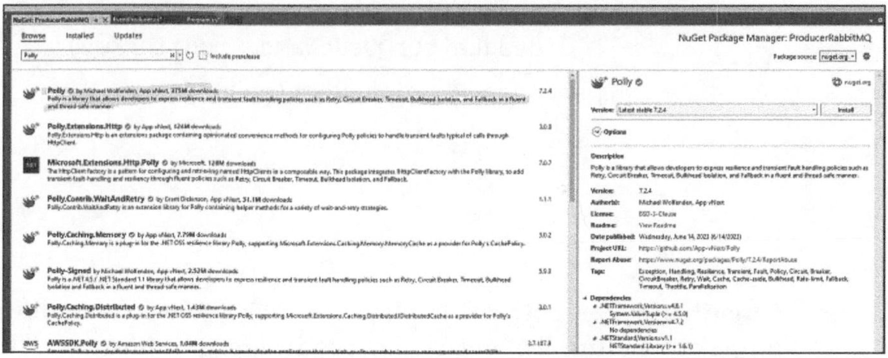

Figure 5.18: Add Polly library using Nuget Package Manager

2. Next, refer to the code snippet of RabbitMQ producers:

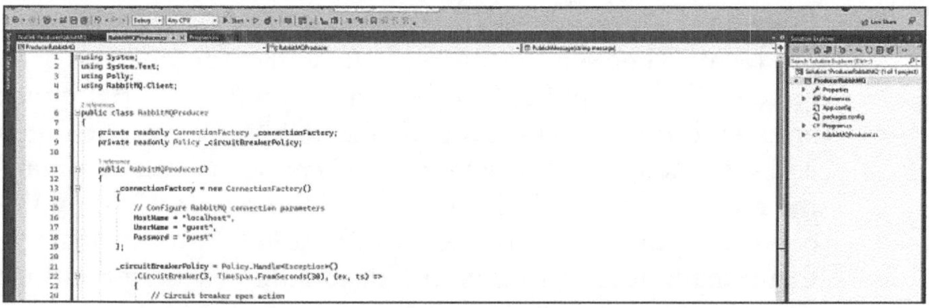

Figure 5.19: Add Event Producer Class EventProducer

3. In the below example, The **RabbitMQProducer** class is utilized to implement the Circuit Breaker Pattern:

```
using System;
using System.Text;
using Polly;
using RabbitMQ.Client;

public class RabbitMQProducer
{
    private readonly ConnectionFactory _
    connectionFactory;
    private readonly Policy _circuitBreakerPolicy;

    public RabbitMQProducer()
    {
```

```
        _connectionFactory = new ConnectionFactory()
        {
            // Configure RabbitMQ connection parameters
            HostName = "localhost",
            UserName = "guest",
            Password = "guest"
        };

        _circuitBreakerPolicy = Policy.Handle<Excep-
        tion>()
            .CircuitBreaker(3, TimeSpan.
            FromSeconds(30), (ex, ts) =>
            {
                // Circuit breaker open action
                Console.WriteLine("Circuit breaker
                opened due to exception: " +
                ex.Message);
            }, () =>
            {
                // Circuit breaker reset action
                Console.WriteLine("Circuit breaker
                reset");
            });
    }

    public void PublishMessage(string message)
    {
        _circuitBreakerPolicy.Execute(() =>
        {
            using (var connection = _connectionFac-
            tory.CreateConnection())
            using (var channel = connection.
            CreateModel())
            {
```

```
                    var body = Encoding.UTF8.Get-
                    Bytes(message);

                    channel.QueueDeclare(queue: "myqueue",
                                         durable: false,
                                         exclusive: false,
                                         autoDelete: false,
                                         arguments: null);

                    channel.BasicPublish(exchange: "",
                                         routingKey:
                                         "myqueue",
                                         basicProperties:
                                         null,
                                         body: body);

                    Console.WriteLine("Message
                    published: " + message);
                }
            });
        }
}
```

In the above code:

- The **RabbitMQProducer** class encapsulates the logic for connecting to RabbitMQ and publishing messages.
- The **_circuitBreakerPolicy** field represents the circuit breaker policy created using Polly. It is configured to open the circuit breaker after three consecutive exceptions within a 30-second window.
- The **PublishMessage** method is where the RabbitMQ connection and message publishing takes place. It is executed within the circuit breaker policy using the Execute method.

4. To use the **RabbitMQProducer** class and publish messages, you can create an instance and call the **PublishMessage** method in Program Class:

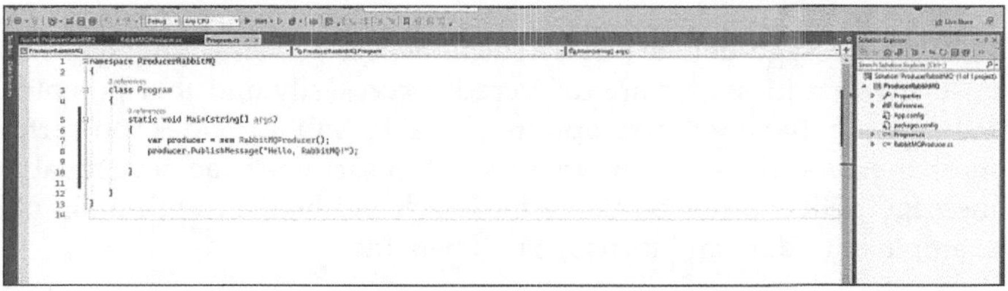

Figure 5.20: Add Program Class to invoke PublishMessage method

5. The below code snippet demonstrates how to use the circuit breaker pattern to handle transient faults in the RabbitMQ producer. If the specified number of exceptions occurs within the defined window, the circuit breaker will open and prevent further message publishing until the circuit breaker resets.

```
namespace ProducerRabbitMQ
{
    class Program
    {
        static void Main(string[] args)
        {
            var producer = new RabbitMQProducer();
            producer.PublishMessage("Hello,
            RabbitMQ!");

        }

    }
}
```

Note: This is a simplified example, and in a real-world scenario, you may need to customize the circuit breaker policy further to handle different types of exceptions and implement fallback or retry mechanisms as needed.

Reliable message delivery using RabbitMQ's

Reliable message delivery is a crucial aspect of messaging systems, ensuring that messages are delivered successfully and that potential failures are handled appropriately. RabbitMQ provides powerful mechanisms such as confirmations and transactions to achieve reliable message delivery. Let us delve into each mechanism with a simple example to understand its usage and benefits.

Confirmations implementation in RabbitMQ

RabbitMQ's confirmations allow publishers to receive acknowledgments from the broker, indicating whether a message has been successfully delivered to the intended destination. This mechanism ensures that publishers can have confidence in the delivery of their messages.

Here is a simple example that demonstrates the usage of confirmations in RabbitMQ:

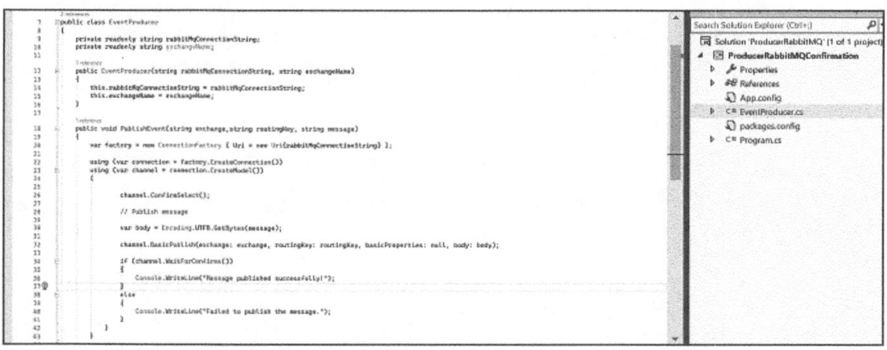

Figure 5.21: Add Event Producer Class EventProducer for Confirmation

In the below figure, the **ConfirmSelect()** method is used to enable publisher acknowledgments on the channel. Once the message is published, **WaitForConfirms()** is employed to await acknowledgments from the broker. If all messages receive acknowledgments successfully, it serves as an indication that the message publication was executed successfully:

```
using RabbitMQ.Client;
```

```
using RabbitMQ.Client.Events;
using System;
using System.Text;
using System.Threading;

public class EventProducer
{
    private readonly string rabbitMqConnectionString;
    private readonly string exchangeName;

    public EventProducer(string rabbitMqConnectionString,
    string exchangeName)
    {
        this.rabbitMqConnectionString =
        rabbitMqConnectionString;
        this.exchangeName = exchangeName;
    }

    public void PublishEvent(string exchange,string
    routingKey, string message)
    {
        var factory = new ConnectionFactory { Uri = new
        Uri(rabbitMqConnectionString) };

        using (var connection = factory.CreateConnection())
        using (var channel = connection.CreateModel())
        {

                channel.ConfirmSelect();

                // Publish message

                var body = Encoding.UTF8.GetBytes(message);

                channel.BasicPublish(exchange: exchange,
                routingKey: routingKey, basicProperties:
```

```
                        null, body: body);

                        if (channel.WaitForConfirms())
                        {
                            Console.WriteLine("Message published
                            successfully!");
                        }
                        else
                        {
                            Console.WriteLine("Failed to publish
                            the message.");
                        }
                    }
                }

}
```

In this example, we create an instance of the **EventProducer** class and call the **PublishEvent** method to publish an event message (refer to the following figure):

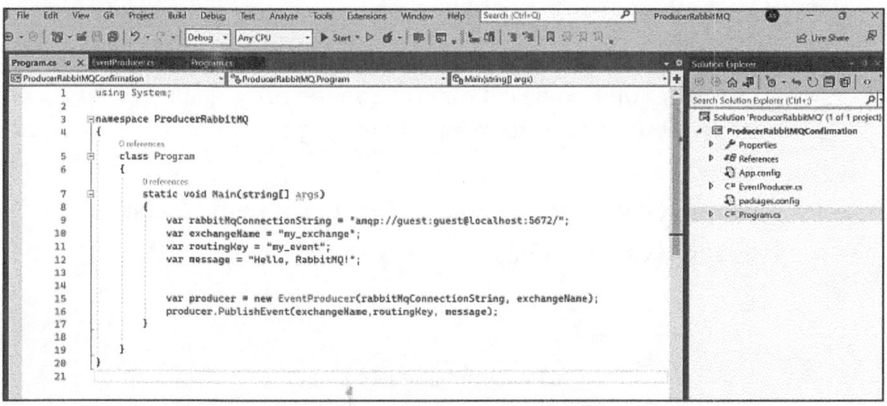

Figure 5.22: Add Program Class to invoke PublishEvent method

The below code implements the **Program** class to invoke the **PublishEvent** method:

```
using System;

namespace ProducerRabbitMQ
{
    class Program
    {
        static void Main(string[] args)
        {
            var rabbitMqConnectionString = "amqp://
            guest:guest@localhost:5672/";
            var exchangeName = "my_exchange";
            var routingKey = "my_event";
            var message = "Hello, RabbitMQ!";

            var producer = new EventProducer(rabbitMqCon-
            nectionString, exchangeName);
            producer.PublishEvent(exchangeName,routingKey,
            message);
        }

    }
}
```

Transactions implementation in RabbitMQ

RabbitMQ's Transactions provide a way to group multiple messaging operations into a single atomic unit. It ensures that either all the operations within the transaction are executed successfully or none of them are executed at all. If any operation fails within a transaction, it can be rolled back to its previous state.

Here is an example illustrating the usage of Transactions in RabbitMQ:

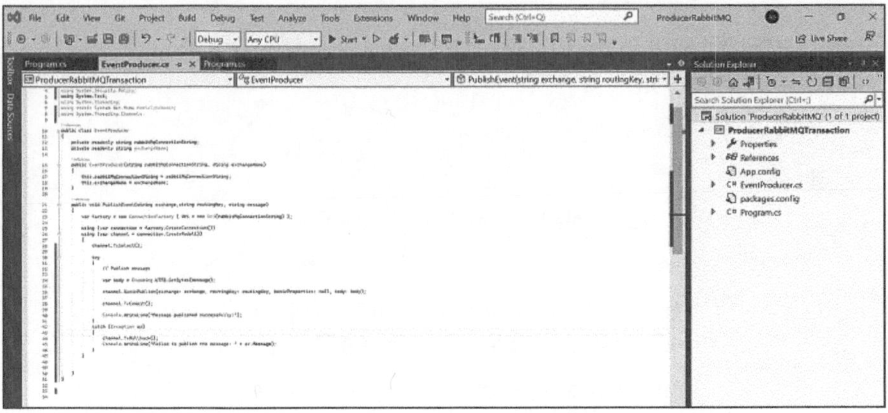

***Figure 5.23:** Add Event Producer Class EventProducer for Transaction*

In this example, the **TxSelect()** method is used to enable transactions on the channel. The message publication operation is wrapped within a try-catch block. If all the operations within the transaction (including message publication) are successful, the transaction is committed using **TxCommit()**. However, if any operation fails, the transaction is rolled back using **TxRollback()** to ensure that no partial changes are made:

```
using RabbitMQ.Client;
using RabbitMQ.Client.Events;
using System;
using System.Security.Policy;
using System.Text;
using System.Threading;
using static System.Net.Mime.MediaTypeNames;
using System.Threading.Channels;

public class EventProducer
{
    private readonly string rabbitMqConnectionString;
    private readonly string exchangeName;

    public EventProducer(string rabbitMqConnectionString,
    string exchangeName)
    {
        this.rabbitMqConnectionString =
```

```
        rabbitMqConnectionString;
        this.exchangeName = exchangeName;
    }

    public void PublishEvent(string exchange,string
    routingKey, string message)
    {
        var factory = new ConnectionFactory { Uri = new
        Uri(rabbitMqConnectionString) };

        using (var connection = factory.CreateConnection())
        using (var channel = connection.CreateModel())
        {
            channel.TxSelect();

            try
            {
                // Publish message

                var body = Encoding.UTF8.GetBytes(message);

                channel.BasicPublish(exchange: exchange,
                routingKey: routingKey, basicProperties:
                null, body: body);

                channel.TxCommit();

                Console.WriteLine("Message published
                successfully!");
            }
            catch (Exception ex)
            {
                channel.TxRollback();
                Console.WriteLine("Failed to publish the
                message: " + ex.Message);
            }
        }
```

```
    }
}
```

By utilizing confirmations and transactions in RabbitMQ, you can ensure reliable message delivery in your applications. Confirmations provide a way to verify successful message delivery, while Transactions allow for atomic operations, ensuring that all or none of the operations take effect. These mechanisms enhance the reliability and robustness of messaging systems built on RabbitMQ.

Conclusion

In conclusion, this chapter has provided a thorough exploration of building event-driven systems with RabbitMQ and .NET. We started by setting up RabbitMQ as a messaging broker, covering the installation, configuration, and defining of message queues and exchanges. We then moved on to implementing event producers using .NET, enabling the generation, and publishing of events. Subsequently, we delved into the implementation of event consumers in .NET, allowing for the subscription to event queues and processing of incoming events.

To ensure reliable message delivery, we discussed error-handling techniques such as retry mechanisms and explored testing strategies like unit testing. We also touched upon monitoring and logging techniques for real-time event analysis. Additionally, we examined deployment options, including local environments and cloud services like Azure or AWS, considering service discovery and load balancing considerations.

By following the practical implementation steps outlined in this chapter, readers can gain a comprehensive understanding of building event-driven systems using RabbitMQ and .NET. This knowledge can be applied to various projects, enabling the development of scalable and resilient systems that leverage the power of event-driven architecture.

The next chapter will delve into implementing essential security measures for event-driven systems. We will focus on authentication and authorization mechanisms to ensure the integrity and access control of event producers and consumers. Additionally, we will explore techniques for encrypting sensitive data within event payloads to protect sensitive information. Secure communication between event producers and consumers will also be discussed, along with implementing log aggregation and analysis for effective event tracing and auditing.

Chapter 6
Secure RabbitMQ Messaging with .NET

Introduction

Building an Event-Driven System with RabbitMQ and .NET will explore the practical implementation of developing event-driven systems. It will give an in-depth understanding of the features and capabilities of RabbitMQ and .NET for building event-driven systems. This implementation will teach you how to set up an Event-Driven System Project in .NET using RabbitMQ libraries.

Structure

In this chapter, we will cover the following topics:

- Authentication for event producers and consumers
- Authorization for event producers and consumers
- Encrypting sensitive data in event payloads
- Log aggregation and analysis for event tracing and auditing

Objectives

This chapter focuses on implementing comprehensive security measures for event-driven systems. It covers a range of objectives, including authentication and authorization mechanisms for event producers and consumers, encryption techniques to safeguard sensitive data within event payloads, and the establishment of log aggregation and analysis for event tracing and auditing. Specific topics include understanding various authentication and authorization mechanisms, configuring authentication for event consumers, setting up a centralized logging infrastructure, and implementing event tracing and auditing mechanisms. By achieving these objectives, the chapter aims to fortify event-driven systems with robust security practices, ensuring data integrity, confidentiality, and compliance.

Authentication for event producers and consumers

Authentication in event-driven architecture with RabbitMQ and .NET is the process of verifying the identity of event producers and consumers. It ensures that only authorized parties can interact with the RabbitMQ event broker, performing actions like publishing or consuming events. By implementing authentication, the system ensures the security and integrity of the event-driven architecture by validating credentials and permissions before granting access to the event broker.

Authentication in event producers

Implementing authentication in event producers involves configuring RabbitMQ to use an authentication mechanism and establishing a connection from the event producer using the appropriate credentials. Here is a detailed step-by-step guide on how to implement authentication in event producers using RabbitMQ and .NET:

- Configure RabbitMQ for authentication:
    - o Ensure that RabbitMQ is configured to use authentication mechanisms.
    - o Create user accounts with appropriate permissions.

- Event producer code:
  - o The **EventProducer** class is responsible for publishing messages to RabbitMQ.
  - o It includes properties such as **_hostname**, **_port**, **_username**, **_password**, **_exchangeName**, and **_routingKey**.
- **ConnectionFactory** configuration:
  - o The **ConnectionFactory** is configured with the RabbitMQ server details and user credentials.
  - o The **UserName** and **password** properties are set with the actual credentials created in RabbitMQ for the event producer.
- Publish message:
  - o Inside the **PublishMessage** method, a **ConnectionFactory** is used to establish a connection to RabbitMQ.
  - o The connection is used to create a channel, and a message is published to the specified exchange (**_exchangeName**) and routing key (**_routingKey**).
- Main method:
  - o The **Program.cs** file contains the entry point for the console application.
  - o An instance of the **EventProducer** is created, and the **PublishMessage** method is called to publish a message.

By following these steps, you configure RabbitMQ for authentication, create user accounts with appropriate permissions, and establish a connection from the event producer using the provided credentials. This ensures that only authorized event producers can interact with RabbitMQ and publish events to the specified exchanges:

// C# coding implementation of the steps explained above:

```
using RabbitMQ.Client;
using System;
using System.Text;

namespace RabbitMQAuthenticationExample
{
```

```
public class EventProducer
{
    private readonly string _hostname = "localhost";
    private readonly int _port = 5672;
    private readonly string _username = "guest";
    private readonly string _password = "guest";
    private readonly string _exchangeName = "my_
    exchange";
    private readonly string _routingKey = "my_routing_
    key";

    public void PublishMessage(string message)
    {
        var factory = new ConnectionFactory()
        {
            HostName = _hostname,
            Port = _port,
            UserName = _username,
            Password = _password
        };

        using (var connection = factory.CreateConnec-
        tion())
        using (var channel = connection.CreateModel())
        {
            var messageBody = Encoding.UTF8.Get-
            Bytes(message);

            channel.BasicPublish(
                exchange: _exchangeName,
                routingKey: _routingKey,
                basicProperties: null,
                body: messageBody
            );
```

```
            }
        }
    }
}
```

In the below given code structure, the **Program.cs** file contains the entry point for the console application, and the **EventProducer.cs** file encapsulates the logic for publishing the message:

```
using System;

namespace RabbitMQAuthenticationExample
{
    class Program
    {
        static void Main(string[] args)
        {
            // Create an instance of the event producer
            var eventProducer = new EventProducer();

            try
            {
                // Publish the message
                eventProducer.PublishMessage("Hello Rab-
                bitMQ");
                Console.WriteLine("Message published suc-
                cessfully!");
            }
            catch (Exception ex)
            {
                Console.WriteLine("Error publishing
                message: " + ex.Message);
            }

            Console.ReadLine();
        }
```

```
    }
}
```

Authentication for event consumers

Authentication in event consumers is the process of verifying the identity and permissions of the consumer before allowing them to access and consume events from the event broker (such as RabbitMQ) in an event-driven architecture. It ensures that only authorized consumers can participate in the event flow.

Here is an explanation of how authentication is typically implemented in event consumers:

- Event consumer code:
    - The **`EventConsumer`** class is responsible for consuming events from RabbitMQ.
    - It includes properties such as **`_hostname`**, **`_port`**, **`_username`**, **`_password`**, **`_exchangeName`**, **`_queueName`**, and **`_routingKey`**.
- **`ConnectionFactory`** configuration:
    - The **`ConnectionFactory`** is configured with the RabbitMQ server details and user credentials.
    - The **`UserName`** and **`Password`** properties are set with the actual credentials created in RabbitMQ for the event consumer.
- Exchange and queue setup:
    - The code sets up the exchange and queue for event consumption.
    - It declares the exchange, declares the queue, and binds the queue to the exchange with the specified routing key.
- Event consumer logic:
    - An **`EventingBasicConsumer`** is created to handle incoming events.
    - The **`Received`** event is subscribed to, which processes and prints the received event message.

- **BasicConsume**:
  - o The **BasicConsume** method is called to start consuming events from the specified queue.
- Main Method:
  - o The **Program.cs** file contains the entry point for the console application.
  - o An instance of the **EventConsumer** is created, and the **Consume**

// C# coding implementation of the steps explained above:

```
using RabbitMQ.Client;
using RabbitMQ.Client.Events;
using System.Text;

namespace RabbitMQAuthenticationExample
{
    public class EventConsumer
    {
        private readonly string _hostname = "localhost";
        private readonly int _port = 5672;
        private readonly string _username = "guest";
        private readonly string _password = "guest";
        private readonly string _exchangeName = "my_
        exchange";
        private readonly string _queueName = "my_queue";
        private readonly string _routingKey = "my_routing_
        key";

        public void ConsumeEvents()
        {
            var factory = new ConnectionFactory()
            {
                HostName = _hostname,
                Port = _port,
                UserName = _username,
```

```
        Password = _password
    };

    using (var connection = factory.CreateConnec-
    tion())
    using (var channel = connection.CreateModel())
    {
        channel.ExchangeDeclare(
            exchange: _exchangeName,
            type: ExchangeType.Direct
        );

        channel.QueueDeclare(
            queue: _queueName,
            durable: true,
            exclusive: false,
            autoDelete: false,
            arguments: null
        );

        channel.QueueBind(
            queue: _queueName,
            exchange: _exchangeName,
            routingKey: _routingKey
        );

        var consumer = new EventingBasicConsum-
        er(channel);
        consumer.Received += (model, eventArgs) =>
        {
            var message = Encoding.UTF8.
            GetString(eventArgs.Body.ToArray());
            Console.WriteLine("Received event: " +
            message);
        };
```

```
                channel.BasicConsume(
                    queue: _queueName,
                    autoAck: true,
                    consumer: consumer
                );

                Console.WriteLine("Waiting for events...");
            }
        }
    }
}
```

When running the console application, the Main method in **Program.cs** creates an instance of the **EventConsumer** class and calls the **ConsumeEvents** method to start consuming events. Any errors encountered during the process are caught and displayed in the console:

```
using System;

namespace RabbitMQAuthenticationExample
{
    class Program
    {
        static void Main(string[] args)
        {
            // Create an instance of the event consumer
            var eventConsumer = new EventConsumer();

            try
            {
                // Consume events
                eventConsumer.ConsumeEvents();
            }
            catch (Exception ex)
```

```
            {
                Console.WriteLine("Error consuming events:
                " + ex.Message);
            }

            Console.ReadLine();
        }
    }
}
```

Authentication is the process of verifying the identity of users or services. In above example, we are using username/password-based authentication to connect to the RabbitMQ server.

In the producer and consumer applications, the authentication details (username, password, virtual host) are provided when creating the `ConnectionFactory` instance.

Authorization for event producers and consumers

Authorization is the process of determining what actions or resources a user or entity is allowed to access after they have been authenticated. It defines the permissions and privileges that a user has based on their identity or roles. Authorization answers the question, *what are you allowed to do?*

In the context of event-driven architecture and RabbitMQ, authorization ensures that the authenticated producer or consumer has the necessary permissions to publish or consume messages from specific queues or exchanges.

Authorization in event producers

Producers are responsible for emitting events to RabbitMQ. Authorization can be implemented to ensure that only trusted and authenticated producers can publish events to specific topics. It plays a crucial role in maintaining the security and integrity of the system, preventing unauthorized access and potential misuse of events. The significance of authorization in EDA can be summarized as follows:

Access control for producers

Authorization mechanisms in EDA control which producers are allowed to publish events to specific topics. This ensures that only trusted and authorized sources can emit events, preventing unauthorized entities from injecting potentially harmful or incorrect information into the system.

Access control is important because of below mentioned reasons:

- **Data privacy**: By enforcing access control for consumers, authorization ensures that sensitive event data is accessible only to authorized microservices, preventing unauthorized access to critical information.
- **Regulatory compliance**: Many industries have strict regulations regarding data privacy and access control. Authorization mechanisms aid in meeting these requirements by controlling access to events and maintaining an audit trail of event-related activities.

Here is a detailed step-by-step guide on how to implement authorization in event producers using RabbitMQ and .NET:

```
using System;
using RabbitMQ.Client;
using System.Text;

namespace EventProducer
{
    public class Producer
    {
        private readonly string _exchangeName;
        private readonly string _routingKey;
        private readonly string _rabbitMQConnectionString;

        public Producer(string exchangeName, string
        routingKey, string rabbitMQConnectionString)
        {
            _exchangeName = exchangeName;
            _routingKey = routingKey;
```

```
        _rabbitMQConnectionString = rabbitMQConnec-
        tionString;
    }

    // Authorization function for publishing events
    public bool IsAuthorizedToPublish(CurrentUser user)
    {
        // Implement your authorization logic here
        based on user's identity or role
        // Return true if the user is authorized to
        publish events, otherwise return false
        // You can use JWT tokens, user roles, or
        any other authentication mechanism to check
        authorization
        return user.HasRole("publisher");
    }

    public void PublishEvent(string message,
    CurrentUser user)
    {
        try
        {
            // Perform authorization check
            if (!IsAuthorizedToPublish(user))
            {
                Console.WriteLine("Not authorized to
                publish events.");
                return;
            }

            var factory = new ConnectionFactory()
            {
                Uri = new Uri(_rabbitMQConnection-
                String),
                DispatchConsumersAsync = true
```

```
        };

        using (var connection = factory.CreateCon-
        nection())
        using (var channel = connection.CreateMod-
        el())
        {
            channel.ExchangeDeclare(_exchangeName,
            ExchangeType.Topic, durable: true,
            autoDelete: false);

            var body = Encoding.UTF8.GetBytes(mes-
            sage);

            var properties = channel.CreateBa-
            sicProperties();
            properties.Persistent = true; // Make
            the message persistent

            channel.BasicPublish(exchange: _ex-
            changeName,
                                 routingKey: _
                                 routingKey,
                                 basicProperties:
                                 properties,
                                 body: body);

            Console.WriteLine(" [x] Sent
            '{0}':'{1}'", _routingKey, message);
        }
    }
    catch (Exception ex)

    {
        Console.WriteLine($"Error publishing
        event: {ex.Message}");
```

```
            }
        }
    }
}
```

In this example, authorization is implemented using a custom method called **IsAuthorizedToPublish(CurrentUser user)**. This method checks if the provided user is authorized to publish events.

The **IsAuthorizedToPublish** method takes a **CurrentUser** object as an argument, which represents the identity of the current user. It is assumed that the **CurrentUser** object contains information about the user's roles or permissions. The method can be customized based on the specific requirements of the system.

Further, the **IsAuthorizedToPublish** method checks if the user has the role **publisher** by calling the **HasRole("publisher")** method on the **CurrentUser** object. If the user has the role **publisher**, the method returns true, indicating that the user is authorized to publish events. Otherwise, it returns false, indicating that the user is not authorized.

The **PublishEvent** method, responsible for publishing the event, first calls the **IsAuthorizedToPublish** method with the **CurrentUser** object as an argument. If the user is not authorized, the method prints a message indicating that the user is not authorized to publish events and returns without publishing the event. If the user is authorized, the method proceeds to publish the event to the specified exchange and routing key.

By combining authentication and authorization, the event producer ensures that only authenticated and authorized users can publish events to RabbitMQ. This helps maintain the security and integrity of the event-driven system, preventing unauthorized access and misuse of events.

Please note that the code provided is a simplified example for demonstration purposes. In a real-world scenario, you would need to implement more robust authentication and authorization mechanisms, such as using JWT tokens, user role management, and secure communication channels, to ensure the security of your event-driven system.

Authorization in event consumers

Implementing authorization in event consumers using RabbitMQ and C# involves a combination of RabbitMQ's access control mechanisms and custom authorization logic in your C# consumer code. RabbitMQ provides robust access control features that allow you to define permissions at the queue and exchange level. Additionally, you can implement custom authorization logic in your consumer code to enforce further restrictions based on your application's requirements.

Authorization checks in code

RabbitMQ's access control mechanism handles most authorization checks. However, you can implement additional authorization logic in your consumer code to enforce more fine-grained access control. For example, based on the authenticated user's roles or claims, you can further decide whether the consumer should process specific types of events.

Handle unauthorized access

If the consumer is not authorized to process a particular event, your consumer code should handle the situation gracefully. It can log the unauthorized access attempt, skip processing the event, or take any other appropriate action based on your application's requirements.

Let us create a C# console application for the event consumer:

```
using System;
using System.Text;
using RabbitMQ.Client;
using RabbitMQ.Client.Events;

namespace EventConsumer
{
    public class EventConsumer
    {
        private readonly string _queueName;
        private readonly string _rabbitMQConnectionString;
```

```
public EventConsumer(string queueName, string
rabbitMQConnectionString)
{
    _queueName = queueName;
    _rabbitMQConnectionString = rabbitMQConnec-
    tionString;
}

public void StartConsuming()
{
    var factory = new ConnectionFactory()
    {
        Uri = new Uri(_rabbitMQConnectionString)
    };

    using (var connection = factory.CreateConnec-
    tion())
    using (var channel = connection.CreateModel())
    {
        channel.QueueDeclare(_queueName, durable:
        true, exclusive: false, autoDelete: false);

        var consumer = new
        EventingBasicConsumer(channel);
        consumer.Received += (sender, ea) =>
        {
            try
            {
                var body = ea.Body.ToArray();
                var message = Encoding.UTF8.
                GetString(body);
                Console.WriteLine("Received
                message: " + message);

                // Implement your authorization
                logic here
```

```
            if
            (IsAuthorizedToProcessMessage(ea.
            BasicProperties.UserId))
            {
                // Process the message here
                Console.WriteLine("Message
                processed successfully.");
                channel.BasicAck(ea.
                DeliveryTag, multiple: false);
                // Acknowledge message
            }
            else
            {
                // Reject or requeue the
                message if not authorized
                Console.WriteLine("Unauthorized
                to process the message.
                Rejecting it.");
                channel.BasicReject(ea.
                DeliveryTag, requeue: false);
            }
        }
        catch (Exception ex)
        {
            Console.WriteLine("Error processing
            message: " + ex.Message);
            channel.BasicReject(ea.DeliveryTag,
            requeue: false);
        }
    };

    channel.BasicConsume(_queueName, autoAck:
    false, consumer);
    Console.WriteLine("Consumer started.
    Waiting for messages...");
```

```
            Console.ReadLine(); // Keep the application
            running until manually stopped.
        }
    }

    private bool IsAuthorizedToProcessMessage(string
    userId)
    {
        // Implement your custom authorization logic
        here based on the user's identity (userId).
        // You can check the user's roles, permissions,
        or any other criteria to determine
        authorization.

        // For demonstration purposes, let's assume
        that any user with a specific role ("consumer")
        is authorized.
        return HasRole(userId, "consumer");
    }

    private bool HasRole(string userId, string roleName)
    {
        // Implement your logic to check if the user
        with the given userId has the specified role
        (roleName).
        // This could involve querying a database or
        an authentication/authorization service.
        // For simplicity, we'll just check if the
        role is "consumer" in this example.
        return roleName.ToLower() == "consumer";
    }
}

class Program
{
    static void Main(string[] args)
```

```
        {
            string queueName = "my_event_queue";
            string rabbitMQConnectionString = "amqp://my_
            consumer:password@localhost:5672/my_virtual_
            host";

            var consumer = new EventConsumer(queueName,
            rabbitMQConnectionString);
            consumer.StartConsuming();
        }
    }
}
```

The **Consumer** class represents our event consumer. It takes the queue name and RabbitMQ connection string in its constructor.

The **StartConsuming** method establishes a connection to RabbitMQ, declares the queue, and sets up a message consumer.

The consumer's **Received** event handler is responsible for processing incoming messages. In this handler, we perform the following steps:

1. Check if the consumer is authorized to process the message by calling the **IsAuthorizedToProcessMessage** method, passing the user's identity as the **UserId** from the message's **BasicProperties**.
2. The **IsAuthorizedToProcessMessage** method implements your custom authorization logic. In this example, we assume that any user with the role **consumer** is authorized.
3. If the user is authorized, we process the message and acknowledge it using **channel.BasicAck**. If the user is not authorized, we reject the message using **channel.BasicReject**, and it will be sent to the dead-letter queue or dropped based on RabbitMQ's configuration.

Please note that the authorization logic provided in this example is simplistic for demonstration purposes. In a real-world scenario, you would likely use a more sophisticated authentication and authorization mechanism, such as JWT tokens, OAuth2, or integration with an identity provider.

Encrypting sensitive data in event payloads

Encrypting sensitive data in event payloads is crucial for ensuring data confidentiality and security when using messaging systems like RabbitMQ to transmit messages between different components or microservices. Encrypting sensitive data ensures that even if an unauthorized entity gains access to the messages, they will not be able to read the sensitive information without the proper decryption key. Here is a detailed explanation of how to encrypt sensitive data in event payloads:

- **Identify sensitive data**: The first step is to identify the data elements within your event payloads that are considered sensitive. Examples of sensitive data could include personal information (e.g., names, addresses), financial information, authentication tokens, or any other data that should remain confidential.
- **Choose encryption algorithm**: AES is efficient for symmetric encryption due to its speed and suitability for large data sets. RSA's strength on the other hand, lies in its asymmetric approach, making it more suitable for encrypting smaller pieces of data, as its computational complexity increases with data size.
- **Generate encryption keys**: For symmetric encryption (e.g., AES), you need to generate a secret encryption key. This key will be used both for encryption and decryption. For asymmetric encryption (e.g., RSA), you need to generate a public-private key pair. The public key is used for encryption, while the private key is used for decryption.
- **Encrypt data**: When sending an event with sensitive data, encrypt the sensitive data using the encryption key before adding it to the event payload. For symmetric encryption, you'll encrypt the data with the same secret key on both the producer and the consumer sides. For asymmetric encryption, you'll encrypt the data with the public key of the recipient (consumer) and ensure that only the recipient has access to the corresponding private key for decryption.
- **Decrypt data**: On the receiving end (event consumer), decrypt the encrypted sensitive data using the appropriate decryption

key (symmetric or private key for asymmetric). The decrypted data can then be safely used and processed by the consumer.

- **Securely manage encryption keys**: Properly manage and protect the encryption keys. Keys should be stored securely, preferably using a **Key Management Service (KMS)** or **Hardware Security Modules (HSMs)**. Restrict access to these keys to authorized personnel only.
- **Implement encryption/decryption logic**: In your event producer and consumer applications, implement the encryption and decryption logic. This may involve using cryptographic libraries provided by your programming language or platform. Be sure to test the encryption and decryption process thoroughly to ensure correctness and performance.
- **Consider performance impact**: Encryption and decryption can add some overhead to message processing. Consider the performance impact and choose appropriate encryption algorithms based on the sensitivity of the data and the required level of security.
- **Handling key rotation**: Periodically rotate encryption keys to minimize the risk of unauthorized access to sensitive data. When rotating keys, ensure that all parties involved (producers and consumers) are aware of the new keys to continue secure communication.
- **Logging and auditing**: Implement proper logging and auditing to track access to sensitive data, including encryption and decryption operations. This is essential for monitoring security and identifying potential security breaches.

By encrypting sensitive data in event payloads, you add an extra layer of protection to ensure the confidentiality and integrity of your data as it travels between different components or services in your distributed system. Encryption is a critical aspect of a comprehensive security strategy, especially when dealing with sensitive information in event-driven architectures.

Let us create a simple example using RabbitMQ and C# to demonstrate how to encrypt and decrypt sensitive data in event payloads.

In this example, we will use symmetric encryption with AES to encrypt and decrypt a sensitive message sent through RabbitMQ. Please note that in a real-world scenario, you should use secure key management and consider using asymmetric encryption for better security:

```
using System;
using System.Linq;
using System.Security.Cryptography;
using System.Text;
using RabbitMQ.Client;
using RabbitMQ.Client.Events;

namespace SecureEventProducer
{
    public class Producer
    {
        private readonly string _queueName;
        private readonly string _rabbitMQConnectionString;
        private readonly byte[] _encryptionKey;

        public Producer(string queueName, string
        rabbitMQConnectionString, byte[] encryptionKey)
        {
            _queueName = queueName;
            _rabbitMQConnectionString =
            rabbitMQConnectionString;
            _encryptionKey = encryptionKey;
        }

        public void PublishSensitiveEvent(string
        sensitiveMessage)
        {
            try
            {
                var encryptedMessage = EncryptMessage(sen-
                sitiveMessage, _encryptionKey);

                var factory = new ConnectionFactory() {
                Uri = new Uri(_rabbitMQConnectionString)
                };
```

```
        using (var connection = factory.
        CreateConnection())
        using (var channel = connection.
        CreateModel())
        {
            channel.QueueDeclare(_queueName,
            durable: true, exclusive: false,
            autoDelete: false);

            var body = Encoding.UTF8.
            GetBytes(encryptedMessage);

            var properties = channel.CreateBa-
            sicProperties();
            properties.Persistent = true; // Make
            the message persistent

            channel.BasicPublish(exchange:
            "", routingKey: _queueName,
            basicProperties: properties, body:
            body);

            Console.WriteLine(" [x] Sent sensitive
            message: " + sensitiveMessage);
        }
    }
    catch (Exception ex)
    {
        Console.WriteLine("Error publishing
        sensitive event: " + ex.Message);
    }
}

private string EncryptMessage(string message,
byte[] key)
{
    using (Aes aesAlg = Aes.Create())
```

```
        {
            aesAlg.Key = key;
            aesAlg.Mode = CipherMode.CBC;
            aesAlg.GenerateIV();

            ICryptoTransform encryptor = aesAlg.
            CreateEncryptor(aesAlg.Key, aesAlg.IV);

            byte[] encrypted;

            using (var msEncrypt = new System.
            IO.MemoryStream())
            {
                using (var csEncrypt = new
                CryptoStream(msEncrypt, encryptor,
                CryptoStreamMode.Write))
                using (var swEncrypt = new System.
                IO.StreamWriter(csEncrypt))
                {
                    swEncrypt.Write(message);
                }
                encrypted = msEncrypt.ToArray();
            }

            byte[] ivAndEncrypted = new byte[aesAlg.
            IV.Length + encrypted.Length];
            Array.Copy(aesAlg.IV, ivAndEncrypted,
            aesAlg.IV.Length);
            Array.Copy(encrypted, 0, ivAndEncrypted,
            aesAlg.IV.Length, encrypted.Length);

           return Convert.ToBase64String(ivAndEncrypted);
        }
    }
}
```

```
public class Consumer
{
    private readonly string _queueName;
    private readonly string _rabbitMQConnectionString;
    private readonly byte[] _encryptionKey;

    public Consumer(string queueName, string
    rabbitMQConnectionString, byte[] encryptionKey)
    {
        _queueName = queueName;
        _rabbitMQConnectionString = rabbitMQConnec-
        tionString;
        _encryptionKey = encryptionKey;
    }

    public void StartConsuming()
    {
        var factory = new ConnectionFactory() { Uri =
        new Uri(_rabbitMQConnectionString) };
        using (var connection = factory.CreateConnec-
        tion())
        using (var channel = connection.CreateModel())
        {
            channel.QueueDeclare(_queueName, durable:
            true, exclusive: false, autoDelete: false);

            var consumer = new EventingBasicConsum-
            er(channel);
            consumer.Received += (sender, ea) =>
            {
                try
                {
                    var body = ea.Body.ToArray();
                    var encryptedMessage = Encoding.
                    UTF8.GetString(body);
```

```
                var decryptedMessage =
                DecryptMessage(encryptedMessage,
                _encryptionKey);

                Console.WriteLine(" [x]
                Received sensitive message: " +
                decryptedMessage);

                channel.BasicAck(ea.DeliveryTag,
                multiple: false); // Acknowledge
                message
            }
            catch (Exception ex)
            {
                Console.WriteLine("Error processing
                message: " + ex.Message);
                channel.BasicReject(ea.DeliveryTag,
                requeue: false);
            }
        };

        channel.BasicConsume(_queueName, autoAck:
        false, consumer);
        Console.WriteLine("Consumer started.
        Waiting for messages...");
        Console.ReadLine(); // Keep the application
        running until manually stopped.
    }
}

private string DecryptMessage(string encryptedMes-
sage, byte[] key)
{
    byte[] ivAndEncrypted = Convert.
    FromBase64String(encryptedMessage);
```

```
        using (Aes aesAlg = Aes.Create())
        {
            aesAlg.Key = key;
            aesAlg.IV = ivAndEncrypted.Take(aesAlg.
            IV.Length).ToArray();

            ICryptoTransform decryptor = aesAlg.
            CreateDecryptor(aesAlg.Key, aesAlg.IV);

            string decryptedMessage;

            using (var msDecrypt = new System.
            IO.MemoryStream(ivAndEncrypted.Skip(aesAlg.
            IV.Length).ToArray()))
            using (var csDecrypt = new
            CryptoStream(msDecrypt, decryptor,
            CryptoStreamMode.Read))
            using (var srDecrypt = new System.
            IO.StreamReader(csDecrypt))
            {
              decryptedMessage = srDecrypt.ReadToEnd();
            }

            return decryptedMessage;
        }
    }
}

class Program
{
    static void Main(string[] args)
    {
        string queueName = "my_event_queue";
        string rabbitMQConnectionString = "amqp://
        guest:guest@localhost:5672/";
```

```
                byte[] encryptionKey = Encoding.UTF8.
                GetBytes("0123456789ABCDEF"); // Replace this
                with a strong encryption key.

                var producer = new Producer(queueName,
                rabbitMQConnectionString, encryptionKey);
                producer.PublishSensitiveEvent("This is a
                sensitive message.");

                var consumer = new Consumer(queueName,
                rabbitMQConnectionString, encryptionKey);
                consumer.StartConsuming();
            }
        }
}
```

Replace the **encryptionKey** variable in the **Program** class with a strong encryption key of your choice. The key should be at least 128 bits (16 bytes) long for AES-128.

Run the application. It will publish a sensitive message using the **Producer** class and then consume and decrypt the message using the **Consumer** class.

Please note that in a real-world scenario, you should use a more robust key management approach and consider using asymmetric encryption for securely sharing encryption keys between producers and consumers.

Log aggregation and analysis for event tracing and auditing

Log aggregation and analysis are crucial components of event tracing and auditing in an event-driven system using RabbitMQ and C#. They enable the centralized collection and analysis of log data generated by different components, allowing system administrators and developers to gain insights into system behavior, troubleshoot issues, and ensure compliance with security and operational policies. Here is a detailed explanation of log aggregation and analysis in such a system:

Log aggregation

Log aggregation involves collecting log data from various sources, such as event producers, consumers, RabbitMQ brokers, and other components within the system, into a centralized repository. This centralized repository is typically a log management system, often referred to as a log aggregator or log collector.

The log aggregator can be a dedicated software solution like the Elastic Stack (Elasticsearch, Logstash, Kibana), Splunk among others. Alternatively, a custom-built solution can be developed to meet specific requirements.

Implementing log aggregation

Steps to implement log aggregation:

1. Configure event producers and consumers to emit log messages with relevant details, including timestamps, log levels, source component, and any other relevant metadata.
2. Direct log messages to a central log storage (e.g., message queues, log files, or log streams).
3. Use appropriate log management software or custom scripts to collect log data from these sources and store them centrally.
4. Employ log rotation and retention policies to manage log storage efficiently.

Log analysis

Once log data is aggregated into the centralized repository, log analysis tools and techniques are used to explore and derive insights from the collected logs. Log analysis is vital for:

- **Troubleshooting and root cause analysis**: Investigating and identifying the causes of errors, exceptions, or performance issues.
- **System performance optimization**: Monitoring system health and identifying areas for improvement.
- **Security monitoring**: Detecting and responding to security incidents and anomalies.
- **Compliance and auditing**: Ensuring adherence to security, operational, and regulatory policies.

Common approaches for log analysis include:

- **Search and filtering**: Use query languages or search tools to filter logs based on specific criteria (e.g., source, severity, time range).
- **Visualization**: Create dashboards and charts to visualize log data, making it easier to spot patterns and anomalies.
- **Alerting**: Set up alerts for specific log patterns or events to receive notifications when critical issues occur.
- **Correlation**: Correlate logs from different sources to understand relationships between events and identify the root cause of issues.

Log analysis in event-driven systems

In event-driven systems using RabbitMQ and C#, log analysis is particularly useful for:

- **Message flow monitoring**: Tracking the flow of events/messages through the system, including message processing times and potential bottlenecks.
- **Error tracking**: Identifying errors and exceptions raised by producers or consumers and pinpointing the component causing the issue.
- **Audit trail**: Ensuring proper auditing of critical operations or sensitive data access.
- **Security monitoring**: Detecting unauthorized access attempts or suspicious behavior.

Security and privacy considerations

Log data can contain sensitive information, such as user identifiers or authentication tokens. Implement measures to protect log data during transit and storage. Encrypt log data in transit using secure communication protocols (e.g., TLS/SSL) and use proper access controls and encryption for log storage.

By employing effective log aggregation and analysis techniques, an event-driven system can gain valuable insights into its operation, ensure compliance with policies, and respond promptly to any issues or security incidents. It enhances the overall observability and manageability of the system.

Let us create a simple example of log aggregation and analysis in a C# event-driven system using RabbitMQ and Splunk for log storage and analysis. In this example, we will use the Serilog library to log messages and the **Serilog.Sinks.Splunk NuGet** package to send log data to Splunk.

1. Install the required NuGet packages:
   - Serilog
   - Serilog.Sinks.Splunk
2. Setup Splunk:

   Install and configure Splunk to receive log data. You can download Splunk from the official website: **https://www.splunk.com/**

```
using System;
using System.Text;
using RabbitMQ.Client;
using RabbitMQ.Client.Events;
using Serilog;
using Serilog.Sinks.Splunk;

namespace EventDrivenLoggingExample
{
    public class Producer
    {
        private readonly string _queueName;
        private readonly string _
        rabbitMQConnectionString;

        public Producer(string queueName, string
        rabbitMQConnectionString)
        {
            _queueName = queueName;
            _rabbitMQConnectionString = rabbitMQCon-
            nectionString;
        }
```

```
public void PublishEvent(string message)
{
    try
    {
        var factory = new ConnectionFacto-
        ry() { Uri = new Uri(_rabbitMQCon-
        nectionString) };
        using (var connection = factory.
        CreateConnection())
        using (var channel = connection.
        CreateModel())
        {
            channel.QueueDeclare(_queueName,
            durable: true, exclusive: false,
            autoDelete: false);

            var body = Encoding.UTF8.
            GetBytes(message);

            var properties = channel.
            CreateBasicProperties();
            properties.Persistent = true; //
            Make the message persistent

            channel.BasicPublish(exchange:
            "", routingKey: _queueName,
            basicProperties: properties,
            body: body);

            Console.WriteLine(" [x] Sent
            message: " + message);
        }
    }
    catch (Exception ex)
    {
        Console.WriteLine("Error publishing
        event: " + ex.Message);
```

```
            }
        }
    }

    public class Consumer
    {
        private readonly string _queueName;
        private readonly string _
        rabbitMQConnectionString;

        public Consumer(string queueName, string
        rabbitMQConnectionString)
        {
            _queueName = queueName;
            _rabbitMQConnectionString =
            rabbitMQConnectionString;
        }

        public void StartConsuming()
        {
            var factory = new ConnectionFactory() {
            Uri = new Uri(_rabbitMQConnectionString)
            };
            using (var connection = factory.
            CreateConnection())
            using (var channel = connection.
            CreateModel())
            {
                channel.QueueDeclare(_queueName,
                durable: true, exclusive: false,
                autoDelete: false);

                var consumer = new EventingBasicCon-
                sumer(channel);
                consumer.Received += (sender, ea) =>
                {
```

```
                try
                {
                    var body = ea.Body.ToArray();
                    var message = Encoding.UTF8.
                    GetString(body);

                    // Log the received message
                    using Serilog
                    Log.Information("Received
                    message: {Message}",
                    message);

                    channel.BasicAck(ea.
                    DeliveryTag, multiple:
                    false); // Acknowledge
                    message
                }
                catch (Exception ex)
                {
                    Console.WriteLine("Error
                    processing message: " +
                    ex.Message);
                    channel.BasicReject(ea.
                    DeliveryTag, requeue:
                    false);
                }
            };

            channel.BasicConsume(_queueName,
            autoAck: false, consumer);
            Console.WriteLine("Consumer started.
            Waiting for messages...");
            Console.ReadLine(); // Keep the
            application running until manually
            stopped.
        }
    }
```

```
    }

    class Program
    {
        static void Main(string[] args)
        {
            string queueName = "my_event_queue";
            string rabbitMQConnectionString =
            "amqp://guest:guest@localhost:5672/";

            // Setup Serilog logger to log to Splunk
            Log.Logger = new LoggerConfiguration()
                .WriteTo.EventCollector("http://
                localhost:8088", "my-token")
                .CreateLogger();

            var producer = new Producer(queueName,
            rabbitMQConnectionString);
            producer.PublishEvent("Hello, this is a
            log message from the producer!");

            var consumer = new Consumer(queueName,
            rabbitMQConnectionString);
            consumer.StartConsuming();

            // Flush the logger before exiting the
            application
            Log.CloseAndFlush();
        }
    }
}
```

Here is an explanation of storing log data in Splunk and how to view it:

1. Replace the Splunk URL (**`http://localhost:8088`**) and token (**`my-token`**) in the Main method with the URL and token of your Splunk instance.

2. Run the application. It will publish a log message from the producer and then consume and log the message using Serilog.
3. Open Splunk in your web browser to view and analyze the logs. You can create visualizations, dashboards, and perform searches and filtering to gain insights from the log data.
4. This example demonstrates a simple implementation of log aggregation and analysis in an event-driven system using RabbitMQ, C#, and Splunk. For a production-ready setup, you would need to consider additional configuration, error handling, and security measures to ensure a robust and secure logging solution.

Conclusion

In conclusion, implementing authentication for event producers and consumers is essential to verify the identities of participants and ensure that only authorized entities can interact with the event-driven system. Authorization mechanisms further control access to specific functionalities or resources based on user roles or permissions, safeguarding sensitive operations and data from unauthorized use. Encrypting sensitive data in event payloads provides a critical layer of protection, ensuring that even if intercepted, the data remains unreadable to unauthorized parties. Log aggregation and analysis, on the other hand, enable comprehensive event tracing and auditing, empowering administrators to monitor system behavior, troubleshoot issues, and maintain compliance with security and operational policies. Together, these security practices foster a robust and secure event-driven architecture, bolstering data privacy, system integrity, and overall reliability.

In the next chapter, you will explore monitoring and management techniques, leveraging tools and libraries to ensure optimal performance and health of the event-driven system, while also managing RabbitMQ server and queues efficiently.

CHAPTER 7

Monitoring, Integration and Deployment in Event-Driven System

Introduction

Monitoring and management tools play a crucial role in assessing the performance and overall health of a system, offering insights into the status of RabbitMQ servers and queues. These tools provide a comprehensive view of system metrics, facilitating proactive measures to ensure optimal functionality. To extend the system's capabilities, integration with external systems and services becomes essential, a task streamlined through technologies like REST and gRPC. These integration methods enable seamless communication and data exchange between diverse components. Furthermore, employing the Event Sourcing and **Command Query Responsibility Segregation (CQRS)** patterns enhances the system's efficiency. By adopting Event Sourcing, data persistence is improved, ensuring a detailed record of system changes over time. Simultaneously, implementing the CQRS pattern segregates the write and read operations, enhancing scalability and overall performance. This combination of monitoring tools, integration technologies, and architectural patterns not only fortifies the system's stability but also lays the foundation for a scalable, responsive, and resilient infrastructure.

Structure

In this chapter, we will cover the following topics:

- Monitoring and management
- Integration with other systems using REST and gRPC
- Event Sourcing and CQRS pattern in Event Driven Architecture
- Microservices and Event Driven Architecture
- Deploying Event Driven System to a cloud environment

Objectives

In this chapter, you will gain insights into how to use tools to maintain your system's health and effectively manage RabbitMQ server and queues. We will also guide you through the process of integrating your event-driven system with external services using techniques like REST and gRPC, which enhances communication. You will also acquire skills in data storage, scalability, and system performance by exploring concepts such as Event Sourcing and CQRS patterns. Additionally, we will introduce you to the microservices approach, enabling independent development of system components. Moreover, you will discover how to deploy your system on the cloud and leverage cloud services for enhanced scalability and reliability. It is important to note, however, that this chapter focuses on a beginner-level understanding, and advanced details are beyond the scope of this book.

Monitoring and management

There are several tools and libraries available for monitoring the performance and health of a RabbitMQ system and for managing the RabbitMQ server and queues. Here are some popular ones:

Monitoring tools and libraries

Monitoring tools and libraries are as follows:

- **Prometheus**: Prometheus is a robust open-source monitoring and alerting toolkit that allows you to gather and analyze metrics from various systems, including RabbitMQ. The RabbitMQ Exporter is a tool that can be integrated with Prometheus to collect metrics from RabbitMQ instances. It exposes metrics in a format that Prometheus can scrape. These metrics cover a wide range of RabbitMQ aspects, such as message rates, queue depths, and connection statistics. Prometheus supports powerful querying capabilities, allowing you to create custom queries and alerts based on RabbitMQ metrics. The integration with visualization tools like Grafana enhances your ability to create insightful dashboards.

- **Grafana**: Grafana is a widely adopted data visualization and monitoring platform. It can connect to Prometheus to display collected RabbitMQ metrics in visually appealing and customizable dashboards. Grafana's intuitive interface enables you to create charts, graphs, and tables that represent RabbitMQ performance data over time. This visualization helps administrators and teams quickly identify trends, anomalies, and potential issues. Grafana's alerting capabilities allow you to set up alerts based on specific RabbitMQ metrics, notifying you when thresholds are breached.
- **RabbitMQ Management Plugin**: RabbitMQ comes equipped with a built-in management plugin that provides a user-friendly web-based interface for monitoring and managing the RabbitMQ server and its components. This plugin offers insights into queue lengths, message rates, connection details, and more. It's an excellent tool for administrators who prefer a graphical interface to monitor the system's health and manage queues, exchanges, and users. The management plugin also allows you to perform tasks like purging queues, tracing messages, and managing user permissions.
- **Datadog**: Datadog is a comprehensive monitoring and analytics platform that supports RabbitMQ monitoring among many other technologies. It offers real-time visibility into RabbitMQ performance, allowing you to track metrics such as message rates, memory usage, and connection counts. Datadog's customizable dashboards enable you to visualize RabbitMQ data alongside other system metrics. Additionally, Datadog provides the ability to set up alerts and notifications based on RabbitMQ metrics, helping you proactively address performance issues. The platform's analytics features allow you to analyze historical data to gain insights into long-term trends and patterns.

These monitoring tools and libraries play a crucial role in ensuring the health and performance of your RabbitMQ system. They enable you to gain a deep understanding of the system's behavior, respond to issues promptly, and optimize its performance for optimal message throughput and reliability. It's worth noting that these tools can be used individually or in combination, depending on your organization's preferences and monitoring requirements.

Management tools and libraries

Managing a RabbitMQ system involves configuring, controlling, and automating various aspects of the server and its components. Here are some tools and libraries that facilitate efficient management:

- **RabbitMQ Admin UI**: The RabbitMQ Management Plugin includes a web-based administrative **user interface (UI)** that provides a convenient and user-friendly way to interact with the RabbitMQ server. It offers a graphical interface for managing queues, exchanges, bindings, users, vhosts, permissions, and more. Through the UI, administrators can easily monitor the state of queues, connections, and exchanges. The interface also allows for interactions such as pausing queues, viewing message details, and triggering various administrative actions. The RabbitMQ Admin UI is particularly useful for those who prefer a visual approach to managing and monitoring their RabbitMQ deployment.
- **RabbitMQctl Command-Line Tool**: RabbitMQ provides a command-line tool called rabbitmqctl that enables administrators to manage and control RabbitMQ from the terminal. With rabbitmqctl, you can perform various administrative tasks, including creating and deleting queues, managing users and permissions, inspecting server status, purging queues, and more. This tool is valuable for administrators who are comfortable working in a command-line environment. It is also useful for scripting and automation purposes, as you can incorporate rabbitmqctl commands into scripts or orchestration tools to automate routine management tasks.
- **RabbitMQ Management HTTP API**: RabbitMQ offers a comprehensive HTTP API that allows for programmatic interaction with the RabbitMQ server. This API provides endpoints for managing virtually every aspect of the RabbitMQ

system, including queues, exchanges, users, virtual hosts, permissions, and more. You can use tools like cURL or libraries in various programming languages (Python, Java, Ruby, etc.) to interact with the API and automate administrative tasks. This approach is beneficial when you need to integrate RabbitMQ management into your application's deployment and configuration processes. It enables you to programmatically create and manage resources, set up users and permissions, and perform various maintenance tasks.

Utilizing these management tools and libraries allows you to maintain the health and performance of your RabbitMQ system effectively. Depending on your preferred workflow and the level of automation you require, you can choose to use the web-based UI, command-line tool, or the HTTP API. Each of these options offers a distinct way to manage RabbitMQ and suits different preferences and use cases. By leveraging these tools, you can streamline administrative tasks, ensure consistency in configurations, and enhance the reliability of your RabbitMQ infrastructure.

Integration with other systems using REST and gRPC

Event-driven systems play a pivotal role in contemporary application architecture, enabling diverse components and services to interact and respond to events with a high degree of flexibility and scalability. Seamlessly incorporating these event-driven systems with other counterparts and services stands as a fundamental requirement for constructing intricate, widely distributed applications. Among the prevalent methods of integration, two widely adopted technologies are **Representational State Transfer (REST)** and gRPC.

Let us delve into the ways in which these technologies expedite the integration process:

- **Integrating with REST**: REST is an architectural style for designing networked applications, emphasizing simplicity, scalability, and statelessness. It is widely used for building APIs that allow different systems to communicate over standard HTTP protocols. Integrating event-driven systems with other systems using REST involves exposing endpoints (APIs) that other services can interact with.

Here is how REST integration works: HTTP Methods: REST APIs use HTTP methods (GET, POST, PUT, DELETE, etc.) to perform actions on resources. For event-driven integration, you can use HTTP POST to send events to a service or resource.

Steps to follow:

- o **Identify event**: Decide which event you want to send or receive. For instance, a "User Registered" event when a new user signs up.
- o **Create an endpoint**: In your service, create an HTTP endpoint (URL) where events will be sent or received. For example, /user-events.
- o **HTTP POST request**: To send an event, make an HTTP POST request to the endpoint with the event data. Use JSON for the event payload.
- o **Receiving events**: Other services can listen to this endpoint to receive events. When an event is received, the service processes it accordingly.

  Example with REST: Sending a "User Registered" event using REST:

```
POST /user-events
Content-Type: application/json

{
  "event": "User Registered",
  "user": {
    "name": "Michael",
    "email": "michael@example.com"
  }
}
```

- **Integrating with gRPC**: gRPC is a high-performance, open-source framework for **remote procedure calls (RPC)** developed by Google. It's designed to enable efficient communication between distributed services, making it a great choice for event-driven integrations. gRPC uses Protocol Buffers as its interface definition language and offers features like authentication, load balancing, and streaming:

- o **Service definitions**: With gRPC, you define services and their methods using Protocol Buffers. These definitions specify the structure of requests and responses.
- o **Bi-directional communication**: gRPC supports both unary and streaming RPCs. Streaming RPCs are particularly useful for event-driven scenarios where services need to exchange multiple messages over time.
- o **Strongly typed interfaces**: gRPC's service definitions provide a strongly typed contract between services, ensuring consistency and accuracy in communication.

Event sourcing and CQRS pattern in Event Driven Architecture

Event sourcing and CQRS often go hand in hand in systems that use events to talk between different parts. Imagine it like a well-coordinated team – events act as signals, triggering different actions, changing things, or sending out notifications. In this setup, Event Sourcing keeps a detailed history of all these changes, while CQRS splits the work of making changes and looking up information. Together, they create a solid foundation for systems that not only track how things evolve over time but also manage who does what in the system. This teamwork boosts the system's ability to adapt, handle more tasks, and work smoothly, creating a well-connected and responsive environment.

Event sourcing

Event sourcing is a software architectural pattern where all changes to an entity's state are captured as an event. These events are then stored in an append-only log, called an event store. The state of an entity can be reconstructed by replaying the events in the event store.

Each event is a small, immutable data structure that encapsulates the details of a state change. When an application needs to retrieve the current state of an entity, it replays the events relevant to that entity from the event store. By applying these events in sequence, the system reconstructs the entity's current state. This approach offers benefits such as auditability, versioning, and the ability to analyze historical data.

Event Sourcing introduces the idea of event-driven architecture at its core, enabling systems to better capture and model business processes, especially those that involve complex workflows, state changes, and distributed communication.

Command Query Responsibility Segregation

Command Query Responsibility Segregation (**CQRS**) is a pattern that separates the responsibilities of handling commands (write operations that change the state) and queries (read operations that retrieve data) into two distinct paths. This separation allows each path to be optimized for its specific task.

In a CQRS architecture, the write path handles incoming commands, such as creating or modifying entities, by applying business logic and generating events. These events are then stored in the event store, and their processing ensures that the system's state is correctly updated.

On the read path, the application retrieves data from read-optimized data stores. These data stores are designed to efficiently serve query requests and present information in a format that suits the querying needs. By separating the read and write paths, CQRS allows each to scale independently, improving performance and responsiveness.

The CQRS pattern is closely related to Event Sourcing because, in many cases, events generated as part of command processing can be used to update read models for querying. This can further enhance the system's ability to provide real-time insights and reporting capabilities.

Advantages of Event Sourcing and CQRS

The advantages of event sourcing and CQRS are:

- **Scalability**: Both patterns allow components of the system to scale independently, enhancing overall performance and responsiveness.
- **Flexibility**: Event Sourcing enables complex business processes to be captured and reconstructed accurately, and CQRS provides tailored data models for different querying needs.

- **Resilience and auditing**: Event Sourcing ensures a complete history of state changes, which can be useful for auditing, debugging, and tracing.
- **Versioning and evolution**: The event-driven approach aligns well with microservices and distributed architectures, allowing for seamless versioning and evolution of services.
- **Real-time insights**: CQRS enhances the ability to provide real-time insights through dedicated read models that cater to specific reporting needs.
- **Consistency and atomicity**: By capturing state changes in events and applying them atomically, Event Sourcing maintains data consistency and offers transactional benefits.

Let us understand the details of Event Sourcing and CQRS by introducing RabbitMQ for event publishing and using C# for the implementation. We'll cover the Event Sourcing and CQRS patterns, along with RabbitMQ, in the context of an e-commerce order management system.

Event sourcing and CQRS with RabbitMQ in C#

// C# sample code for implementing Event Sourcing and CQRS with RabbitMQ.

In this enhanced example, the `EventPublisher` class is responsible for publishing events to RabbitMQ. The `OrderService` and `ShippingService` classes handle placing and shipping orders by generating and publishing events. On the command side, `PlaceOrderCommandHandler` and `ShipOrderCommandHandler` process the commands and publish relevant events.

On the query side, `GetOrderDetailsQueryHandler` reconstructs the order's state by querying events from the event store and returns the order details.

```
// NuGet package: RabbitMQ.Client
using RabbitMQ.Client;


// Event representing an order being placed
class OrderPlacedEvent
```

```
{
    public int OrderId { get; set; }
    public int CustomerId { get; set; }
    public List<OrderItem> Items { get; set; }
    public decimal TotalAmount { get; set; }
}

// Event representing an order being shipped
class OrderShippedEvent
{
    public int OrderId { get; set; }
    public DateTime ShippingDate { get; set; }
}

// Publishing events using RabbitMQ
class EventPublisher
{
    private IConnection _connection;
    private IModel _channel;

    public EventPublisher()
    {
        var factory = new ConnectionFactory() { HostName =
        "localhost" };
        _connection = factory.CreateConnection();
        _channel = _connection.CreateModel();
        _channel.QueueDeclare(queue: "events_queue",
        durable: false, exclusive: false, autoDelete:
        false, arguments: null);
    }

    public void PublishEvent(object eventData)
    {
```

```
        var jsonEventData = JsonConvert.SerializeOb-
        ject(eventData);
        var body = Encoding.UTF8.GetBytes(jsonEventData);
        _channel.BasicPublish(exchange: "", routingKey:
        "events_queue", basicProperties: null, body: body);
    }

    public void Dispose()
    {
        _channel.Close();
        _connection.Close();
    }
}

// Placing an order
class OrderService
{
    private EventPublisher _eventPublisher;

    public OrderService(EventPublisher eventPublisher)
    {
        _eventPublisher = eventPublisher;
    }

    public void PlaceOrder(int orderId, int customerId,
    List<OrderItem> items)
    {
        decimal totalAmount = CalculateTotalAmount(items);
        var orderPlacedEvent = new OrderPlacedEvent {
        OrderId = orderId, CustomerId = customerId, Items
        = items, TotalAmount = totalAmount };
        _eventPublisher.PublishEvent(orderPlacedEvent);
    }
}
```

```
// Shipping an order
class ShippingService
{
    private EventPublisher _eventPublisher;

    public ShippingService(EventPublisher eventPublisher)
    {
        _eventPublisher = eventPublisher;
    }

   public void ShipOrder(int orderId, DateTime shippingDate)
    {
        var orderShippedEvent = new OrderShippedEvent {
        OrderId = orderId, ShippingDate = shippingDate };
        _eventPublisher.PublishEvent(orderShippedEvent);
    }
}
```

// C# code for CQRS with RabbitMQ

```
// Command to place an order
class PlaceOrderCommand
{
    public int OrderId { get; set; }
    public int CustomerId { get; set; }
    public List<OrderItem> Items { get; set; }
}

// Command to ship an order
class ShipOrderCommand
{
    public int OrderId { get; set; }
    public DateTime ShippingDate { get; set; }
}
```

```
// Query to get order details
class GetOrderDetailsQuery
{
    public int OrderId { get; set; }
}

// Command handler for placing an order
class PlaceOrderCommandHandler
{
    private EventPublisher _eventPublisher;

    public PlaceOrderCommandHandler(EventPublisher
    eventPublisher)
    {
        _eventPublisher = eventPublisher;
    }

    public void Handle(PlaceOrderCommand command)
    {
        decimal totalAmount = CalculateTotalAmount(command.
        Items);
        var orderPlacedEvent = new OrderPlacedEvent {
        OrderId = command.OrderId, CustomerId = command.
        CustomerId, Items = command.Items, TotalAmount =
        totalAmount };
        _eventPublisher.PublishEvent(orderPlacedEvent);
    }
}

// Command handler for shipping an order
class ShipOrderCommandHandler
{
    private EventPublisher _eventPublisher;
```

```
    public ShipOrderCommandHandler(EventPublisher
    eventPublisher)
    {
        _eventPublisher = eventPublisher;
    }

    public void Handle(ShipOrderCommand command)
    {
        var orderShippedEvent = new OrderShippedEvent {
        OrderId = command.OrderId, ShippingDate = command.
        ShippingDate };
        _eventPublisher.PublishEvent(orderShippedEvent);
    }
}

// Query handler for getting order details
class GetOrderDetailsQueryHandler
{
    public OrderDetails Handle(GetOrderDetailsQuery query)
    {
        var state = ReconstructState(query.OrderId);
        return state;
    }
}
```

This combined usage of Event Sourcing, CQRS, and RabbitMQ allows for a scalable and maintainable architecture, where commands and queries are separated, and events are used to communicate changes and updates.

However, the adoption of Event Sourcing and CQRS introduces certain challenges:

- **Complexity**: Implementing Event Sourcing and CQRS can add complexity to the application, requiring a design that can effectively store and process events.

- **Data Volume**: Event Sourcing increases data volume since all state changes are captured as events, potentially impacting storage requirements.
- **Cost**: The patterns may lead to increased costs due to the additional infrastructure needed for event storage and processing.

The decision to utilize Event Sourcing and CQRS in an event-driven architecture hinges on the application's specific requirements. If scalability, fault tolerance, and auditability are paramount, these patterns offer significant benefits. On the other hand, if these features are not crucial, the complexity and cost incurred by these patterns might outweigh their advantages. Careful consideration of the trade-offs is essential in making an informed architectural decision.

Microservices and Event-Driven Architecture

Microservices and **event-driven architecture (EDA)** are two distinct, but complementary architectural concepts often used together to build flexible and scalable software systems. In this explanation, I'll clarify how microservices can be understood in the context of event-driven architecture.

Microservices architecture

Microservices architecture is an approach to software development where an application is divided into a collection of small, loosely coupled services, each responsible for a specific business capability. These services operate independently and communicate with each other through well-defined APIs, such as HTTP/REST, gRPC, or message brokers. The key characteristics of microservices include:

- **Decomposition**: Breaking down a monolithic application into smaller, manageable services, often aligned with specific business functions.
- **Independence**: Each microservice has its own data storage, business logic, and may even have its own user interface. This independence allows for flexibility in development and deployment.

- **Inter-service communication**: Microservices communicate with each other to achieve complex functionalities. They can use various communication patterns, including synchronous (HTTP) and asynchronous (messaging) communication.
- **Scalability**: Microservices can be individually scaled based on their specific resource needs, allowing efficient resource allocation.
- **Resilience**: Microservices are designed to handle failures gracefully, ensuring that a failure in one service does not bring down the entire application.
- **Continuous deployment**: Each microservice can be developed, tested, and deployed independently, resulting in shorter development cycles.

Microservices in Event-Driven Architecture

Microservices can be closely integrated with event-driven architecture to achieve certain advantages:

- **Decoupled communication**: Microservices can communicate with each other asynchronously through events. This decoupling allows services to evolve independently, as they are not tightly bound to the real-time availability of other services.
- **Scalability**: Event-driven communication can help achieve horizontal scalability by allowing services to consume events as their processing capacity allows. This is particularly useful for services that experience varying workloads.
- **Flexibility**: Microservices can subscribe to events that are relevant to their responsibilities. This means that when a particular microservice needs to respond to an event, it can do so without requiring immediate action from other services.
- **Real-time updates**: Event-driven communication enables real-time updates and event-based triggers. For example, an e-commerce system can notify the shipping service to prepare an order for shipment as soon as the "OrderPlaced" event is received.

- **Event-driven microservices patterns**: Architectural patterns such as Event Sourcing and **Command Query Responsibility Segregation (CQRS)** are often employed in microservices to manage state changes and data retrieval through events.

In summary, microservices architecture and event-driven architecture are complementary approaches that, when combined, can provide flexibility, scalability, and decoupled communication in the development of complex software systems. Microservices can be thought of as the individual building blocks that, when integrated with event-driven communication, create a dynamic and responsive ecosystem of services capable of handling a wide range of business scenarios.

How to implement a microservices architecture

Implementing a microservices architecture for an e-commerce application using RabbitMQ and C# involves designing and developing several microservices that work together through event-driven communication. Below, we look at a detailed example and sample code for the core components of this system:

E-commerce Microservices Architecture overview

For our example, let us consider four essential microservices in an e-commerce application:

- **Product service**: Responsible for managing product information.
- **Order service**: Handles order placement and processing.
- **User service**: Manages user registration and authentication.
- **Payment service**: Handles payment processing.

We will use RabbitMQ to facilitate communication between these services through events:

- **Setting-up RabbitMQ**: Before implementing the microservices, you need to set up RabbitMQ and configure exchanges and queues. Please refer to *Chapter 4, Implementing Event-driven Architecture with RabbitMQ and .NET* for installation process.

- **Product Service (Microservice 1):** The Product Service manages product information. It responds to queries for product details and updates product availability.

```
// Sample code for Product Service

using RabbitMQ.Client;

var factory = new ConnectionFactory() { HostName =
"localhost" };
using (var connection = factory.CreateConnection())
using (var channel = connection.CreateModel())
{
    // Declare an exchange for publishing product
    events
    channel.ExchangeDeclare("product_exchange",
    ExchangeType.Fanout);

    // Handle incoming product requests
    channel.QueueDeclare("product_queue", durable:
    false, exclusive: false, autoDelete: false);
    channel.QueueBind("product_queue", "product_
    exchange", "");

   var consumer = new EventingBasicConsumer(channel);
    consumer.Received += (model, ea) =>
    {
        // Handle product-related events (e.g.,
        ProductAdded, ProductUpdated)
        var message = Encoding.UTF8.GetString(ea.
        Body);
        ProcessProductEvent(message);
    };
    channel.BasicConsume(queue: "product_queue",
    autoAck: true, consumer: consumer);

    // Publish a product event (e.g., when a new
```

```
        product is added)
        var productEvent = new ProductAddedEvent {
        ProductId = 123, Name = "Example Product" };
        var messageBody = Encoding.UTF8.
        GetBytes(Serialize(productEvent));
        channel.BasicPublish(exchange: "product_
        exchange", routingKey: "", basicProperties:
        null, body: messageBody);
}
```

- **Order Service (Microservice 2)**: The Order Service handles order placement and processing. It listens for order-related events and processes them accordingly.

```
// Sample code for Order Service

using RabbitMQ.Client;

var factory = new ConnectionFactory() { HostName =
"localhost" };
using (var connection = factory.CreateConnection())
using (var channel = connection.CreateModel())
{
    // Declare an exchange for publishing order events
    channel.ExchangeDeclare("order_exchange",
    ExchangeType.Fanout);

    // Handle incoming order requests
    channel.QueueDeclare("order_queue", durable:
    false, exclusive: false, autoDelete: false);
    channel.QueueBind("order_queue", "order_
    exchange", "");

    var consumer = new EventingBasicConsumer(channel);
    consumer.Received += (model, ea) =>
    {
        // Handle order-related events (e.g.,
        OrderPlaced, OrderProcessed)
```

```
        var message = Encoding.UTF8.GetString(ea.
        Body);
        ProcessOrderEvent(message);
    };
    channel.BasicConsume(queue: "order_queue",
    autoAck: true, consumer: consumer);

    // Publish an order event (e.g., when an order
    is placed)
    var orderEvent = new OrderPlacedEvent { OrderId
    = 456, TotalAmount = 100.00m };
    var messageBody = Encoding.UTF8.
    GetBytes(Serialize(orderEvent));
    channel.BasicPublish(exchange: "order_exchange",
    routingKey: "", basicProperties: null, body:
    messageBody);
}
```

- **User Service (Microservice 3):** The User Service handles user registration and authentication. It listens for user-related events and processes them.

```
// Sample code for User Service

using RabbitMQ.Client;

var factory = new ConnectionFactory() { HostName =
"localhost" };
using (var connection = factory.CreateConnection())
using (var channel = connection.CreateModel())
{
    // Declare an exchange for publishing user events
    channel.ExchangeDeclare("user_exchange",
    ExchangeType.Fanout);

    // Handle incoming user requests
    channel.QueueDeclare("user_queue", durable:
    false, exclusive: false, autoDelete: false);
```

```
    channel.QueueBind("user_queue", "user_exchange",
    "");

    var consumer = new EventingBasicConsumer(channel);
    consumer.Received += (model, ea) =>
    {
        // Handle user-related events (e.g.,
        UserRegistered, UserLoggedIn)
        var message = Encoding.UTF8.GetString(ea.
        Body);
        ProcessUserEvent(message);
    };
    channel.BasicConsume(queue: "user_queue",
    autoAck: true, consumer: consumer);

    // Publish a user event (e.g., when a new user
    registers)
    var userEvent = new UserRegisteredEvent { UserId
    = 789, Username = "example_user" };
    var messageBody = Encoding.UTF8.
    GetBytes(Serialize(userEvent));
    channel.BasicPublish(exchange: "user_exchange",
    routingKey: "", basicProperties: null, body:
    messageBody);
}
```

- **Payment service (Microservice 4):** The Payment Service handles payment processing. It listens for payment-related events and processes them.

```
// Sample code for Payment Service

using RabbitMQ.Client;

var factory = new ConnectionFactory() { HostName =
"localhost" };
using (var connection = factory.CreateConnection())
using (var channel = connection.CreateModel())
```

```
{
    // Declare an exchange for publishing payment
    events
    channel.ExchangeDeclare("payment_exchange",
    ExchangeType.Fanout);

    // Handle incoming payment requests
    channel.QueueDeclare("payment_queue", durable:
    false, exclusive: false, autoDelete: false);
    channel.QueueBind("payment_queue", "payment_
    exchange", "");

    var consumer = new EventingBasicConsumer(channel);
    consumer.Received += (model, ea) =>
    {
        // Handle payment-related events (e.g.,
        PaymentReceived, PaymentFailed)
        var message = Encoding.UTF8.GetString(ea.
        Body);
        ProcessPaymentEvent(message);
    };
    channel.BasicConsume(queue: "payment_queue",
    autoAck: true, consumer: consumer);

    // Publish a payment event (e.g., when a payment
    is received)
    var paymentEvent = new PaymentReceivedEvent {
    OrderId = 456, Amount = 100.00m };
    var messageBody = Encoding.UTF8.
    GetBytes(Serialize(paymentEvent));
    channel.BasicPublish(exchange: "payment_
    exchange", routingKey: "", basicProperties:
    null, body: messageBody);
}
```

- **Event handling**: Each microservice listens for events specific to its responsibilities and processes them. You should implement event handlers like `ProcessProductEvent`, `ProcessOrderEvent`, `ProcessUserEvent`, and `ProcessPaymentEvent` to perform the necessary actions based on the received events.
- **Error handling and retry**: Implement error handling and retry mechanisms for event processing to ensure resilience. You can use libraries like Polly for implementing retry policies and Circuit Breaker patterns for handling failures.
- **Scaling**: Depending on the workload and traffic patterns, you may need to scale your microservices horizontally by deploying multiple instances behind a load balancer.
- **Monitoring and Logging**: Implement monitoring and logging to track the flow of events and troubleshoot issues. Tools like Prometheus, Grafana, and the ELK stack can be helpful for monitoring and log analysis.
- **Testing**: Thoroughly test your microservices and the event-driven architecture to ensure they function as expected. Consider unit tests, integration tests, and end-to-end tests for different scenarios.

In this example, we have demonstrated how to implement a simple e-commerce microservices architecture using RabbitMQ and C#. Each microservice communicates through events, allowing them to work independently while maintaining loose coupling. This architecture promotes scalability, resilience, and maintainability, which are crucial for building robust e-commerce applications.

Deploying Event Driven System to a cloud environment

Deploying an event-driven system to a cloud environment using RabbitMQ, C#, and Azure involves several steps and components. Event-driven systems are designed to handle asynchronous communication between different parts of an application or between different applications. RabbitMQ is a message broker that facilitates this communication, while C# is a commonly used language for building applications. Azure provides a cloud environment for hosting and managing your event-driven system.

Here is a detailed guide on how to deploy such a system:

1. **Design your event-driven system**: Before deploying your system, you should have a clear design in mind. Define the events, message formats, and the components that will interact with each other through RabbitMQ.

2. **Set up your Azure Environment**:
   a. **Create an Azure Account**: If you do not already have one, sign up for an Azure account.
   b. **Create a Resource Group**: Organize your Azure resources by creating a resource group.

3. **Provision Azure resources**:
   a. **Azure Virtual Machines (VMs):** Deploy one or more VMs to host your C# applications.
   b. **Azure Storage**: Use Azure Blob Storage or Azure Table Storage for storing application data if needed.
   c. **Azure Key Vault (optional)**: Securely store sensitive information like connection strings, secrets, and keys.

4. **Install and configure RabbitMQ**:
   a. **Create a RabbitMQ Cluster**: Deploy RabbitMQ on one or more VMs within your Azure environment. You can use a tool like RabbitMQ Cluster on Azure Marketplace or set it up manually.
   b. **Configure RabbitMQ**: Set up virtual hosts, users, permissions, and queues as per your design.

5. **Develop C# applications**:
   a. **Publisher Applications**: These applications generate events and publish them to RabbitMQ. Use the RabbitMQ .NET client library to send messages.
   b. **Consumer applications**: These applications subscribe to events from RabbitMQ and process them accordingly. Again, use the RabbitMQ .NET client library to consume messages.

6. **Secure your applications:**
    a. **Azure Active Directory (Azure AD):** Implement Azure AD for authentication and authorization.
    b. **SSL/TLS:** Secure your RabbitMQ connections using SSL/ TLS certificates.
7. **Deploy C# applications:**
    a. Package your C# applications and deploy them to the Azure VMs you provisioned earlier.
    b. Ensure your applications can connect to RabbitMQ and other Azure services.
8. **Monitor and debug:**
    a. Implement logging and monitoring using Azure Application Insights, Azure Monitor, or similar tools.
    b. Use RabbitMQ management tools or monitoring plugins to keep an eye on RabbitMQ's health and message traffic.
9. **Scale and load balancing (optional):**
    a. Set up load balancing for your C# applications to distribute traffic evenly.
    b. Consider auto-scaling mechanisms based on traffic patterns.
10. **Testing:**
    a. Thoroughly test your system to ensure that events are published, consumed, and processed correctly.
    b. Simulate different scenarios, including failures and high loads.
9. **Backup and disaster recovery (optional):** Implement backup and disaster recovery strategies for RabbitMQ, Azure resources, and your C# applications.
10. **Documentation and maintenance:**
    a. Document the deployment process, configurations, and procedures.
    b. Establish a maintenance plan to apply updates, patches, and scaling adjustments as needed.

11. **Monitoring and optimization**:
    a. Continuously monitor the system's performance and resource utilization.
    b. Optimize your applications and infrastructure based on usage patterns.
12. **Security updates**: Keep all software and libraries, including RabbitMQ, C#, and Azure services, up to date to address security vulnerabilities.
13. **Compliance and Governance (Optional)**: Ensure your system complies with any industry-specific regulations or organizational governance requirements.

Deploying an event-driven system to Azure with RabbitMQ and C# is a complex but rewarding endeavor. It enables your applications to communicate efficiently and asynchronously while taking advantage of cloud scalability and reliability. Make sure to follow best practices for each component and continuously monitor and optimize your system for the best performance and user experience.

Conclusion

In conclusion, this chapter provides a thorough overview of key **event-driven architecture (EDA)** topics. We explored critical aspects like monitoring, underlining real-time insights' importance, and discussed the pivotal role of REST and gRPC integration for seamless system connectivity. We delved into Event Sourcing and the CQRS pattern's role, enabling scalable, resilient EDA systems with microservices synergy. The benefits of deploying Event-Driven Systems in the cloud, leveraging scalability and reliability, were emphasized. These concepts form a robust foundation for designing modern software systems.

In the next chapter, we'll explore real-world scenarios illustrating the impact of RabbitMQ and .NET in event-driven systems. Case studies will highlight the transformative effect of asynchronous messaging, emphasizing scalability and fault tolerance. We'll delve into best practices, offering insights on performance optimization, caching, and load balancing for efficient event-driven architecture implementation. Additionally, common pitfalls in RabbitMQ and .NET within event-driven ecosystems will be scrutinized, with pragmatic strategies provided for readers to navigate challenges and craft resilient systems using these technologies.

CHAPTER 8

Case Studies, Pitfalls and Future Horizons

Introduction

Case studies are real-life examples that show how a system or technology is used. They help us understand the problems faced, how they were solved, and what happened as a result.

Best practices are like a set of tips and rules based on a lot of experience in an industry. They help to set up a system or technology in the best way possible to reach certain goals. They can be changed to fit the needs of different organizations.

Structure

In this chapter, we will cover the following topics:

- Case study: Implementing Event-Driven Architecture
- Real-world examples of event-driven systems using RabbitMQ and .NET
- Optimizing performance and scalability
- Revisiting fundamental EDA concepts

- Common pitfalls and how to avoid them
- Future developments in Event-Driven Architecture

Objectives

The chapter thoroughly explores RabbitMQ and .NET's practical applications in event-driven systems across industries, showcasing specific use cases and their real-world functionalities. It not only highlights successful applications but also addresses challenges during implementation, offering strategies for identification and resolution. Emphasizing scalable solutions, data consistency, and error handling, it guides practitioners in bypassing common pitfalls. Additionally, it provides a forward-looking perspective on event-driven architecture, analyzing emerging trends and potential technological advancements. This foresight offers insights into future developments, keeping readers informed about the evolving tech landscape. Moreover, it compiles various learning materials for a deeper understanding of event-driven architecture using RabbitMQ and .NET, comprising book references, courses, documentation, forums, and tools for continual expertise development.

Case studies: Implementing Event-Driven Architecture

Event-driven architecture (EDA) has become a popular choice for building modern, scalable, and resilient applications. .NET, with its rich ecosystem and mature libraries, combined with the powerful message broker RabbitMQ, provides a fantastic combination for implementing EDA. Let us explore some real-world case studies showcasing how different organizations leveraged this powerful duo.

Case studies: Order processing system in e-commerce platform

Imagine an e-commerce platform that experiences a surge in orders during special events or promotions. To efficiently handle the increased load and ensure a seamless ordering process, the company decides to transition its monolithic order processing system to an event-driven architecture.

Problem statement

The existing monolithic architecture struggles to scale during peak order times, leading to delays and potential order failures. The company aims to improve scalability, resilience, and maintainability by embracing an event-driven architecture.

Sequence diagram

The below figure illustrates the relation between objects, showing the message exchanged in the order of occurrence:

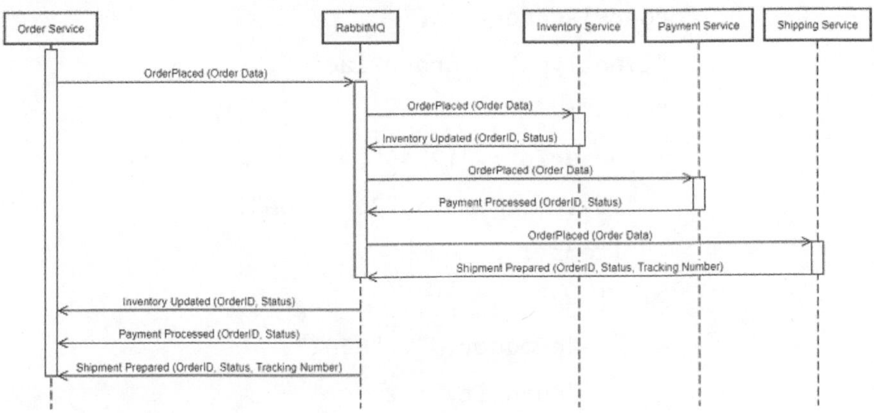

***Figure 8.1:** Sequence diagram*

Architecture design

The new architecture involves breaking down the monolithic order processing system into smaller, independent microservices that communicate through events. The system consists of the following components:

- **Order service activation:**
  - o The sequence begins with the activation of the `Order Service`.

    Sample JSON Schema:

```
{
  "orderServiceActivation": {
    "eventType": "activation",
```

```
    "serviceName": "Order Service"
  }
}
```

- **Order placement**:
  - The **`Order Service`** sends an **`"OrderPlaced"`** message containing order data to RabbitMQ.

    Sample JSON Schema:

```
{
  "orderPlacement": {
    "eventType": "orderPlaced",
    "data": {
      "orderId": "12345",
      "customerName": "John Doe",
      "items": [
        {
          "productId": "P001",
          "quantity": 2
        },
        {
          "productId": "P002",
          "quantity": 1
        }
      ]
    }
  }
}
```

- **RabbitMQ activation**:
  - RabbitMQ is activated upon receiving the "**`OrderPlaced`**" message from the Order Service.

    Sample JSON Schema:

```
{
```

```
        "rabbitMQActivation": {
          "eventType": "activation",
          "serviceName": "RabbitMQ"
        }
    }
```

- **Inventory service activation**:
    - o RabbitMQ forwards the **"OrderPlaced"** message to the **Inventory Service**.
    - o The **Inventory Service** processes the message and responds with an **"Inventory Updated"** message containing **OrderID** and **Status** back to RabbitMQ.

    Sample JSON Schema:

```
{
  "inventoryServiceActivation": {
    "eventType": "activation",
    "serviceName": "Inventory Service"
  }
}

{
  "inventoryUpdated": {
    "eventType": "inventoryUpdated",
    "data": {
      "orderId": "12345",
      "status": "processed"
    }
  }
}
```

- **Payment service activation**:
    - o RabbitMQ forwards the **"OrderPlaced"** message to the **Payment Service**.

- o The **Payment Service** processes the message and responds with a **"Payment Processed"** message containing **OrderID** and **Status** back to RabbitMQ.

  Sample JSON Schema:

```
{
  "paymentServiceActivation": {
    "eventType": "activation",
    "serviceName": "Payment Service"
  }
}

{
  "paymentProcessed": {
    "eventType": "paymentProcessed",
    "data": {
      "orderId": "12345",
      "status": "success"
    }
  }
}
```

- **Shipping service activation**:
  - o RabbitMQ forwards the **"OrderPlaced"** message to the **Shipping Service**.
  - o The **Shipping Service** processes the message and responds with a **"Shipment Prepared"** message containing **OrderID**, **Status**, and **Tracking Number** back to RabbitMQ.

    Sample JSON Schema:

```
{
  "shippingServiceActivation": {
    "eventType": "activation",
    "serviceName": "Shipping Service"
```

```
    }
  }

  {
    "shipmentPrepared": {
      "eventType": "shipmentPrepared",
      "data": {
        "orderId": "12345",
        "status": "ready",
        "trackingNumber": "TRK123"
      }
    }
  }
```

- **Update Order Service**:
  - RabbitMQ sends messages back to the **`Order Service`** informing it about the updates from other services:
    - **`"Inventory Updated"`** with **`OrderID`** and **`Status`**.
    - **`"Payment Processed"`** with **`OrderID`** and **`Status`**.
    - **`"Shipment Prepared"`** with **`OrderID`**, **`Status`**, and **`Tracking Number`**.

  Sample JSON Schema:

```
{
  "updateOrderService": {
    "eventType": "updateOrderService",
    "data": [
      {
        "eventType": "inventoryUpdated",
        "data": {
          "orderId": "12345",
          "status": "processed"
        }
```

```
            },
            {
              "eventType": "paymentProcessed",
              "data": {
                "orderId": "12345",
                "status": "success"
              }
            },
            {
              "eventType": "shipmentPrepared",
              "data": {
                "orderId": "12345",
                "status": "ready",
                "trackingNumber": "TRK123"
              }
            }
          ]
        }
      }
```

Technology stack

RabbitMQ is chosen as the message broker to facilitate communication between the microservices. The microservices are developed using the .NET framework, leveraging technologies like ASP.NET Core for the web services and RabbitMQ client for interacting with RabbitMQ.

Implementation details

- The **`Order Service`** sends an "**OrderPlaced**" event to the RabbitMQ message broker upon receiving a valid order.
- The **`Inventory`**, **`Payment`**, and **`Shipping`** services subscribe to the **`"OrderPlaced"`** event on RabbitMQ.
- Upon receiving the event, each service performs its specific task, such as updating inventory, processing payments, and preparing shipments.

Use cases and scenarios

- During a promotional event, the system efficiently handles a sudden influx of orders, as each microservice scales independently based on demand.
- If the `Inventory Service` encounters issues, it can be taken offline for maintenance without affecting the other services, ensuring high availability.

Challenges and solutions

Challenge 1: Ensuring the consistency of order processing across multiple services.

Solution: Implementing compensating transactions and leveraging RabbitMQ's durability features to handle potential failures.

Challenge 2: Managing the order of events and avoiding race conditions.

Solution: Using RabbitMQ's message queue to maintain the order of events and employing appropriate locking mechanisms.

Results and outcomes

- Improved system scalability and responsiveness during peak times.
- Enhanced fault tolerance, with the ability to recover from service failures without impacting the entire system.

Lessons learned

- Effective monitoring and logging are crucial for identifying and resolving issues in an event-driven system.
- Thorough testing of each microservice's interactions is essential to ensure seamless integration.

The adoption of event-driven architecture using RabbitMQ, and the .NET framework has significantly improved the e-commerce platform's ability to handle increased order volumes, ensuring a smooth and scalable ordering process during special events and promotions.

Real-world examples of event-driven systems using RabbitMQ and .NET

Real-world applications of event-driven systems utilizing RabbitMQ, and .NET showcase their functionality across various industries:

- **E-commerce**: In the e-commerce domain, RabbitMQ plays a pivotal role in promptly responding to customer orders. When a customer places an order on an e-commerce platform, a RabbitMQ event is triggered, notifying the order processing service. Despite high order volumes, this system ensures immediate event consumption and order processing, guaranteeing swift customer responses.
- **Financial services**: Within financial services, RabbitMQ serves in real-time transaction processing and fraud detection. Banks leverage RabbitMQ to publish events when customers conduct transactions, enabling services to swiftly update account balances, detect fraudulent activities, and promptly alert customers. This real-time approach aids in fraud prevention and enhances transaction efficiency.
- **Gaming**: RabbitMQ finds application in gaming for real-time multiplayer gameplay and game analytics. For instance, when a player engages in actions like moving characters or attacking others, RabbitMQ events are generated. Other players subscribing to these events update their gameplay, fostering a synchronized and interactive gaming experience.
- **Social media**: Platforms like social media extensively rely on RabbitMQ for real-time feeds and notifications. When users post updates, messages, or engage with content, RabbitMQ events are distributed. Subscribed users receive instant feed updates or notifications, facilitating timely interactions and content consumption.

  Moreover, prominent companies effectively leverage RabbitMQ and .NET in their event-driven systems:

- **Netflix**: The renowned streaming platform uses RabbitMQ for its real-time recommendation system. When users watch content, RabbitMQ events trigger notifications to update recommendation algorithms, enhancing user experience through tailored suggestions.

- **Twitter**: This social media giant utilizes RabbitMQ for real-time feeds and notifications. When a user posts a tweet, RabbitMQ events inform followers, ensuring immediate updates to their feeds.
- **Amazon**: The e-commerce giant employs RabbitMQ to handle order processing. When customers place orders, RabbitMQ events notify various services such as inventory and shipping, ensuring seamless order processing.

These applications highlight the versatility of event-driven systems, offering benefits like scalability, resilience, and loose coupling. RabbitMQ's reliability, scalability, and user-friendly features make it a preferred choice. Meanwhile, .NET serves as a robust platform for constructing sophisticated event-driven systems. Overall, these examples demonstrate the robustness and adaptability of RabbitMQ and .NET in diverse, real-world event-driven scenarios.

Optimizing performance and scalability

Optimizing performance and scalability in an event-driven architecture is crucial for ensuring that the system can handle increasing loads, maintain responsiveness, and deliver a high-quality user experience.

Here are detailed explanations of key strategies to optimize performance and scalability in EDA:

- **Message compression and serialization**: Compressing and efficiently serializing messages can significantly reduce the size of messages transmitted across the system. This minimizes network overhead and improves overall performance.

  Its benefits are reduced bandwidth usage, faster message transmission.
- **Asynchronous processing**: Leveraging asynchronous processing for handling events allows systems to continue processing other tasks while waiting for event responses. This improves resource utilization and responsiveness.

Its benefits are improved concurrency, responsiveness, and resource efficiency.

- **Load balancing**: Distributing incoming event traffic across multiple instances of event consumers helps prevent bottlenecks and ensures that the load is evenly distributed.

  Its benefits are scalability, fault tolerance, and efficient resource utilization.

- **Horizontal scaling**: Scaling out by adding more instances of event consumers or producers horizontally across multiple servers or containers. This approach increases the system's capacity to handle a higher volume of events. Its benefits are improved scalability, increased throughput, and redundancy.

- **Partitioning and sharding**: Dividing the event data into partitions or shards allows for parallel processing and storage. Each partition can be processed independently, enhancing overall scalability.

  Its benefits are improved parallelism, reduced contention, and increased throughput.

- **Caching**: Introducing caching mechanisms, either at the event producer or consumer side, can reduce the need to repeatedly process the same data. This is particularly useful for frequently accessed or static data.

  Its benefits are reduced latency, improved response times, and optimized resource usage.

- **Latest optimized database access**: Carefully designing and optimizing database access patterns can have a significant impact on overall system performance. This includes indexing, query optimization, and efficient data retrieval strategies.

  Its benefits are a faster data access, improved database performance.

- **Batch processing for bulk operations**: For scenarios involving bulk data operations or updates, batching multiple events into a single process can be more efficient than processing each event individually.

  Its benefits are reduced overhead, improved efficiency for bulk operations.

- **Monitoring and profiling**: Implementing robust monitoring and profiling tools allows for the identification of performance bottlenecks and areas of improvement. This includes monitoring message queues, event processing times, and resource usage.

Its benefits are proactive issue detection, performance optimization insights.

- **Auto-scaling**: Implementing auto-scaling mechanisms allows the system to dynamically adjust the number of resources based on demand. This ensures that the system can handle varying workloads efficiently.

  Its benefits are adaptive scalability, and cost optimization.

- **Optimized Event Schema**: Designing efficient and compact event schemas reduces the size of transmitted messages, resulting in lower processing and transmission times.

  Its benefits are that it has reduced bandwidth usage, faster message processing.

- **Backpressure handling**: Implementing mechanisms to handle backpressure is crucial for preventing overload. This involves signaling producers to slow down or stop sending events when consumers are unable to keep up.

  The benefits are that it prevents resource exhaustion and maintains system stability.

By implementing these strategies, developers and architects can enhance the performance and scalability of event-driven architectures, ensuring that they can efficiently handle increasing workloads while maintaining responsiveness and reliability. Continuous monitoring and optimization are key to adapting to changing demands and ensuring the long-term success of the system.

Revisiting fundamental EDA concepts

Let us revisit some fundamental concepts in **event-driven architecture (EDA)**:

- **Event**: An event is a significant change or occurrence in a system that is of interest to the system or its stakeholders. Events represent a state transition and can trigger reactions or processes within the system.

- **Event producer**: An event producer is a component or system that generates and emits events. It is responsible for publishing events to the event bus, making them available for other components to consume.
- **Event consumer**: An event consumer is a component or system that subscribes to and processes events. It reacts to the occurrence of specific events and performs actions based on the information received.
- **Event bus**: The event bus is a communication channel or infrastructure that facilitates the exchange of events between event producers and event consumers. It acts as a mediator, ensuring that events are delivered to the appropriate consumers.
- **Publish-subscribe pattern**: In the publish-subscribe pattern, event producers publish events to the event bus, and event consumers subscribe to receive specific types of events. This pattern enables loose coupling between producers and consumers.
- **Event handler**: An event handler is a component responsible for processing and responding to a specific type of event. It contains the logic or code that executes when the associated event occurs.
- **Command Query Responsibility Segregation (CQRS):** CQRS is a design pattern that advocates separating the read and write operations of a system. It uses different models for handling commands (write operations) and queries (read operations), enhancing scalability and flexibility.
- **Event-driven microservices**: Event-driven microservices architecture involves building microservices that communicate asynchronously through events. Each microservice is an independent entity that reacts to events and can be developed, deployed, and scaled independently.
- **Event sourcing**: Event sourcing is a pattern where the state of a system is determined by a sequence of events. Instead of storing the current state, the system reconstructs it by replaying events. This approach provides a complete audit trail of changes.
- **Dead letter channel:** A dead letter channel is a mechanism for handling events that cannot be delivered to their intended

consumers. Instead of discarding these events, they are routed to a dead letter channel for analysis and potential reprocessing.

- **Sagas**: Sagas are a pattern for managing distributed transactions in an event-driven system. A saga represents a sequence of smaller, independent transactions that participate in an overall business process.
- **Idempotence**: Idempotence ensures that processing a message multiple times has the same effect as processing it once. This property is crucial for maintaining consistency in event-driven systems, especially when dealing with retries or reprocessing.

Revisiting these fundamental concepts helps maintain a solid understanding of the principles that govern event-driven architecture. These concepts provide the foundation for designing scalable, resilient, and loosely coupled systems that leverage the benefits of event-driven communication.

Common pitfalls and how to avoid them

Event-driven architecture (EDA) is a software design pattern that decomposes an application into loosely coupled components that communicate with each other by asynchronously publishing and subscribing to events. EDA offers several benefits, such as scalability, resilience, and flexibility. However, there are also some common pitfalls that can be avoided when implementing EDA.

Here are some common pitfalls and how to avoid them for event-driven architecture:

Pitfall 1: Not understanding the domain: Before implementing EDA, it is important to have a good understanding of the business domain and the requirements of the system. This includes understanding the different types of events that will be published and consumed, as well as the relationships between the different components of the system. Without this understanding, it is difficult to design an effective EDA system.

How to avoid it:

- Spend time with business stakeholders to understand the domain and requirements.

- Create a domain model that captures the different types of events and relationships between components.
- Use event storming to identify and define business events.

Pitfall 2: Not using a consistent event schema: Events should be published and consumed using a consistent schema. This makes it easier to develop and maintain the system, and it also helps to prevent errors.

How to avoid it:

- Define a consistent event schema for all events published and consumed in the system.
- Use versioning for event schemas so that consumers can handle changes in a controlled manner.
- Use a tool or library to help you generate and validate events according to the schema.

Pitfall 3: Not using idempotent consumers: Consumers should be idempotent, meaning that they can safely process the same event multiple times without producing any unintended side effects. This is important to prevent data corruption and other problems.

How to avoid it:

- Design your consumers to be idempotent. This can be done by using a message queue to store events and ensuring that consumers only process each event once.
- Use a distributed transaction manager to coordinate transactions across multiple services.

Pitfall 4: Not handling errors gracefully: Consumers should handle errors gracefully. This can be done by retrying failed messages, logging errors, or publishing error events.

How to avoid it:

- Implement a retry mechanism for consumers so that they can automatically retry failed messages.
- Log errors to a central repository so that they can be investigated and resolved.
- Publish error events so that other components in the system can be notified of errors.
- By avoiding these common pitfalls, you can build event-driven systems that are scalable, resilient, and reliable.

Pitfall 5: Assuming the network is secure: Relying on the assumption that the network is inherently secure can lead to vulnerabilities, exposing sensitive information to unauthorized access during event transmission.

How to avoid it:

Implement secure communication protocols such as encryption and authentication. Assume that the network is potentially insecure and take necessary security measures like securing data in transit.

Pitfall 6: Ignoring transport cost: Neglecting the cost associated with transporting events over the network can lead to inefficient resource utilization and impact the overall performance of the system.

How to avoid it:

Consider the cost implications of network usage, especially in scenarios where events need to be transmitted over long distances. Optimize the event delivery mechanism to minimize unnecessary expenses.

Pitfall 7: Assuming a homogeneous network: If the network has a consistent and homogeneous environment can lead to compatibility issues when dealing with diverse systems or different network conditions.

How to avoid it:

Design the event-driven system to be adaptable to heterogeneous network environments. Consider variations in network conditions, protocols, and technologies that might be encountered in different parts of the system.

Here are some additional tips for implementing EDA successfully:

- Use an event bus to decouple the production and consumption of events.
- Design your system for asynchronous communication.
- Use consistent event naming and schemas.
- Make sure your consumers are idempotent.
- Use dead-letter queues to collect and handle failed messages.
- Implement a robust error handling strategy.
- Monitor your system closely and be prepared to scale it up or down as needed.

Future developments in event-driven architecture

Here are some of the future developments in event-driven architecture:

- **Standardization of event formats and protocols**: This would make it easier to interoperate between different event-driven systems. Some work is already being done in this area, such as the CloudEvents specification.
- **Evolution of event-driven streaming platforms**: These platforms provide a way to ingest, process, and store events in real time. As these platforms continue to evolve, they will become more scalable, reliable, and efficient.
- **Increased use of event-driven APIs**: Event-driven APIs are APIs that expose events as resources or operations that can be accessed by clients. This type of API is becoming increasingly popular, as it allows developers to build more responsive and scalable applications.
- **Adoption of event-driven serverless computing**: Serverless computing is a cloud computing model where the cloud provider manages the server infrastructure. Event-driven serverless computing platforms allow developers to build event-driven applications without having to worry about managing servers.
- **Edge computing and IoT:** As edge computing gains momentum, EDA plays a crucial role in processing and reacting to real-time data generated by IoT devices. This trend demands low-latency, distributed event processing capabilities.
- **Improved Latency**: The redesigned implementation also optimizes message processing and delivery, resulting in lower latency for MQTT communication. This can be crucial for real-time applications requiring fast message exchange.
- **Use of artificial intelligence and machine learning to improve event-driven systems**: AI and machine learning can be used to improve event-driven systems in several ways, such as:
    - Identifying patterns and anomalies in event data.
    - Predicting future events and taking proactive action.
    - Automating the deployment and management of event-driven systems.

These are just some of the future developments in event-driven architecture. As EDA continues to mature, it is likely that we will see even more innovative and ground-breaking applications of this technology.

Here are some specific examples of how these future developments could be used to improve event-driven systems:

- A standardized event format could be used to make it easier for different event-driven systems to interoperate. This could enable new applications, such as real-time event aggregation and filtering.
- An event-driven streaming platform could be used to ingest and process events in real time to power a real-time fraud detection system.
- An event-driven API could be used to expose events from a **Customer Relationship Management (CRM)** system to a marketing automation system. This would allow the marketing automation system to send personalized messages to customers based on their recent activity.
- An event-driven serverless computing platform could be used to build a real-time social media feed. When a user posts a new update, an event would be published to the serverless computing platform. The platform would then trigger a function to process the event and update the user's social media feed.
- AI and machine learning could be used to identify patterns and anomalies in event data to detect fraud or other suspicious activity. AI and machine learning could also be used to predict future events and take proactive action, such as scaling up a system to handle an expected increase in traffic.

These are just a few examples of how future developments in event-driven architecture could be used to improve event-driven systems. As EDA continues to mature, we can expect to see even more innovative and ground-breaking applications of this technology.

Conclusion

In conclusion, RabbitMQ and .NET exemplify robust event-driven systems, showcasing their efficacy in various real-world applications. They streamline communication and enhance scalability. However, common pitfalls, such as message loss and system complexities, can be mitigated through diligent error handling and proper monitoring. Looking ahead, future developments in event-driven architecture promise advancements in event sourcing, serverless computing, and increased adoption of event mesh technologies. Embracing these changes and focusing on fault-tolerance, security, and improved integration will ensure more resilient, efficient, and adaptive event-driven systems for the evolving technological landscape.

Join our book's Discord space

Join the book's Discord Workspace for Latest updates, Offers, Tech happenings around the world, New Release and Sessions with the Authors:

https://discord.bpbonline.com

Index

D

E

F

G

H

I

K

L

M

N

O

P

Q